Baseball's Greatest Hits & Misses

Baseball's Greatest Hits & Misses

AMAZING TO ZANY FACTS

Jack L. Hayes

Other books by Jack L. Hayes

Business Fraud: From Trust to Betrayal

Baseball's Finest Moments

Baseball's Archives 1845 – 1959

The Power of 2 — Jump Start Your Business

Dedication

I am grateful to so many people—too many for space to allow—who have helped me along life's way. However, to those four individuals who have had the most positive impact on helping me set my personal and professional directions, I proudly dedicate this book:

First, to my late Mom and Dad, who had the foresight and motivation to take me out of a small coal-mining town in West Virginia to much greater opportunities in Washington, D. C. They taught me the extreme importance of honesty and integrity.

To the late Clark C. Griffith, former owner of the Washington Senators baseball club (1920–1955). "The Old Fox" took a telephone call from this unknown 13-year-old kid, listened to my request, and through his efforts I was given the greatest job a kid could ever have! I became the visiting team's batboy when the Washington Senators played at Griffith Stadium. Imagine what it was like to rub elbows with some of the greatest players of all time, including Mickey Mantle, Satchel Paige, Ted Williams, and dozens of other immortal stars.

To my beautiful wife, Darlene who is always there to help and encourage me in everything I do—certainly not because I think that I should, but because **I want to!**

Contents

Introduction

"It's a beautiful day for a ballgame; let's play two!"

—*Ernie Banks, Chicago Cubs*

I recently stopped by my favorite book store. In the sports section, I found book-after-book about Major League Baseball (MLB) players—Hank Aaron, Joe DiMaggio, Mickey Mantle, Satchel Paige, Ted Williams, Ty Cobb, Willie Mays, Lou Gehrig, and almost every book imaginable about Babe Ruth, and numerous others. All players, who in one way or another, left their mark on the game. Those bookshelves appeared to sage from the weight of so many books. I wondered why so many anthologies on baseball?

The obvious answer: the sport has so much to offer writers and readers. I have published two books on baseball. It's time for me to write my third book about my favorite sport. With more than a century of history, the game is filled with many great and exciting stories, including those little nuggets and traditions that don't go down in the record books. The ones that happen in the dugout, the locker-room, or on the field, even in the stands. For me, no other books on sports are as entertaining as those written on baseball.

I started writing this book the day I trotted onto the baseball field at Griffith Stadium in Washington, D.C. It was April 16, 1953 and I was wearing the uniform of the World Champion New York Yankees! My dream had come true. At the age of thirteen, I had become the batboy for the visiting team, whenever the American League's Washington Senators played at Griffith Stadium. For two years, I *"worked"* with and wore the uniform of each of the seven American League teams that visited Griffith Stadium. I rubbed elbows with some of the game's most talented players, and was also privy to hearing several incredible stories of baseball's past. Team managers, coaches, and players held me spellbound with their tales during those special times we spent together in the clubhouse, the dugout, and on the field during batting practice.

My story actually came to life here at...

Griffith Stadium, Washington, D.C.

As a major league batboy, I made Griffith Stadium my second home. I loved that old ballpark. However, to get to the stadium wasn't so easy. I rode the streetcar across town from southeast Washington to the upper northwest side. I estimate that I made this trek 170 times. But still, I was one lucky kid!

I learned quickly that while Major League Baseball is packed with history, it is also loaded with surprises. I was fortunate to see a number of incredible events take place directly in front of me: a few fielding plays that will likely never be duplicated, several home runs that can only be described as spectacular, plus a few other heart-wrenching undertakings. Some of them were hilarious, some sad, some downright dumb, but that's baseball!

Today as I write, I am sad. Three days ago we lost one of baseball's greatest, most colorful and caring legends of all time, Yogi Berra. I met Yogi in 1953.

He was fun to be around, told great stories about the past, and the two of us enjoyed sharing and trading comic books. Once in a while, Yogi would deliver some line that would grab everyone's attention, like "*I didn't say everything I said.*"

Yogi Berra became an almost instant and respected friend. I never heard anyone say a single negative thing about Yogi. He was not only an extremely talented player, he was exceptionally kind and caring—rare qualities in the world of sports. Yogi Berra will be sorely missed!

No other sport comes close to matching the number of surprising and inconceivable things that have taken place throughout Major League Baseball's many decades of play. In this book I share with you some of those nuggets I picked up along the way, and a few other amazing *Hits and Misses*—unconventional, bizarre, wacky, and legendary happenings that took place on and off a big league baseball field. Furthermore, if you are not interested in being bombarded with statistics, you will be pleased to find that I refer to statistics only to make a point or two about a specific player or event.

This book is filled with amazing true accounts of situations—from A to Z, from *amazing* to *zany*. I think you'll have fun with this book.

Nostalgia is important to baseball. It allows each of us to bring back fond recollections of some of the game's most memorable and exciting moments. Join me in reminiscing about this all-American sport.

Jack L. Hayes

Batter up!

CHAPTER ONE
Spectacular Home Runs

"It's going, going, gone."

—Mel Allen

The home run is perhaps the most exciting feat in all of baseball. When the slugger connects and delivers the mighty power that sends that long ball deep into the stands or over a fence, it's magic.

In the early 1900s, the "Dead Ball Era" in baseball, home runs as we know them today were rare. The distances to fences or stands were often too far for a well-hit ball to reach. For example, at Boston Braves Field, the distance down the lines measured over 400 feet and was nearly 500 feet to dead center; the Chicago Cubs' West Side Grounds, 560 feet to the center field fence; the Boston Red Sox's Huntington Avenue Grounds, 635 feet to the center field fence; and at the Philadelphia Athletics' Shibe Park, the distance to the center field fence was 515 feet.

Even if the distances to the parks' perimeters had been reachable, the poor condition of the baseballs in play almost guaranteed that powerful hitters would fail at any attempt to "go for the fences." Most balls were kept in the game for 100 pitches or more, even if lopsided, lumpy, dirty, or "dead." That was until a MLB player was killed by a pitch in 1920.

Along with better baseballs and safer pitching rules, came Babe Ruth and his mighty swing. This new combination changed baseball forever. The sport shifted from a strategic, low-scoring, speed-dominated game to one that was built around the hitter's power as it evolved into an exciting and high-scoring event. Baseball fans loved this new era of excitement; the game's popularity and attendance increased significantly.

The events related in this chapter are not about the longest home runs ever hit, nor the most impactful, but each contributed plenty to the game, as did the men who hit them, and will live forever in the annals of Major League Baseball.

Shot Heard 'Round the World'

In mid-August 1951, the New York Giants trailed the first-place Brooklyn Dodgers by thirteen and one-half games, and Dodgers' manager Charlie Dressen had announced, "The Giants is dead." Dressen's proclamation appeared to be a jinx for his team as the Dodgers commenced to lose game after game and the Giants came to life. The Giants went on a 16-game winning streak on August 12th that ended on August 28th. By the season's final weekend, the Giants had not only tied the Dodgers for the National League's lead, they had forced a three-game playoff to determine which team—Dodgers or

Giants— would advance to play the American League's New York Yankees in the World Series.

The Giants won the playoff opener, 3-1, at Ebbets Field, behind Thomson's two-run homer off Branca, the Dodgers starter. The next day at the Polo Grounds, the Dodgers crushed the Giants 10-0. On Wednesday, October 3, 1951, the two teams met to play their third and final game of the National League playoffs. The winner would advance to the World Series. Millions of viewers were expected to watch the first major league game ever televised nationwide. Millions more would be listening to the game on the radio, including thousands of American servicemen tuned in on the Armed Forces Radio network.

Crowd anticipation and excitement, spurred on by the deep-rooted, cross-town rivalry between the New York Giants and the Brooklyn Dodgers, set the stage for an epic game. Over the last few weeks of the regular season, the Giants had claimed an unbelievable string of victories over the first place Dodgers, winning 37 of their last 44 games to force a three-game playoff series to decide the National League's championship.

Excitement? You bet there was excitement! On television, the game moved along at a decent pace, and when this third and deciding game went into the top of the eighth inning—the two teams were tied 1-1. But not for long! The Dodgers came to life. They scored three runs, giving the Dodgers a comfortable 4-1 lead before the inning was over.

The Giants went down in order in the bottom of the eighth, and their pitching staff did not allow any Dodgers runs in the top of the ninth. Hope for the Giants was rapidly vanishing; it was now their final time at-bat. With a comfortable three-run advantage, the Dodgers sensed a win as did their fans. They were now only three outs from victory, and a trip to the World Series. Let the celebrations begin! But...in the words of Yogi Berra, *"The game ain't over till it's over!"*

Up first in the bottom of the ninth was Giants shortstop, Alvin Dark. With the score 4-1 he singled. Don Mueller hit a single and Dark moved from first to third. Monte Irvin popped out, but Whitely Lockman drove a double down the left field line, scoring Dark and advancing Mueller to third. Unfortunately for Mueller, he broke his ankle during his hard slide into third. Clint Hartung replaced him as a pinch runner.

What unfolded next was one of the most thrilling instances in organized baseball, often cited by players and historians alike as Major League Baseball's most memorable moment... ever!

With the New York Giants down by two, Bobby Thomson stepped into the batter's box. On the mound was Dodgers pitcher Ralph Branca. The count worked to no balls and one strike. Branca wound up and delivered his next pitch, a high fastball; Thomson swung and connected. The crowd was on its feet.

"There's a long drive...it's gonna be...I believe..the Giants win the pennant! The Giants win the pennant! The Giants win the pennant! The Giants win the pennant! Bobby Thomson hits into the lower deck of the left-field stands! The Giants win the pennant, and they're going crazy, they're going crazy. I don't believe it, I don't believe it, I do not believe it!"

Announcer Russ Hodges was shouting into the microphone. The Sporting News christened this single event the greatest moment in baseball history. *Sports Illustrated* ranked this spectacular ending as the second-greatest sports moment of the 20th century (only after the U.S. hockey team's victory over the Soviet Union in the 1980 Olympics).

Blemish or black-eye?

Thomson's three-run homer brought a stirring conclusion to the New York Giants' late-summer comeback that became known as the "Miracle of Coogan's Bluff." Naturally, Bobby Thomson was the Giants' hero! However, years later, Dave Anderson of *The New York Times* in his book *Pennant Races* (1994), told of allegations that the 1951 Giants had conducted a signal stealing operation at the time of Thomson's home run. Not to be outdone, reporter Joshua Prager wrote a similar article in *The Wall Street Journal* in 2001 and followed up again in his book *The Echoing Green* (2006) by reporting that several players on the Giants' 1951 team, including Thomson, had confirmed that they stole opposing catchers' signals for much of the season via a buzzer system using a "spy" with a telescope in the center-field clubhouse at the Polo Grounds. Thomson allegedly told Prager that he was not tipped-off to the kind of pitch Branca would be throwing when he hit his pennant-winning homer. In an interview, Ralph Branca said he felt that Thomson did receive a signal from the Giants' bullpen that a fastball was coming on that fateful pitch. "When you took signs all year, and when you had a chance to hit a bloop or hit a home run, would you ignore that sign?" Branca said. "He knew it was coming. Absolutely!"

Tape-Measure Homer

As a kid, I had a saying, "If you don't swing the bat, you can't hit the ball." Mostly, I used those words to motivate myself into going after things that I considered practically unachievable—sometimes my saying paid off, other times, it didn't. My greatest dream in the early '50s was to become a major league batboy. Unfortunately, I did not know a single person, even remotely connected to professional baseball. But I believed and never let my dream die.

In 1953, my dream came true!

On Friday afternoon, April 17, 1953, my second day at "work" as visiting team batboy for the New York Yankees at Griffith Stadium in Washington, D.C., little did I know that this day would not only go down in baseball history, but also take its place in the *Guinness Book of World Records*.

MICKEY MANTLE'S TITANIC 565 FOOT HOME RUN

In the top of the fifth inning, batting right-handed, Mickey Mantle of the Yankees stepped into the batter's box to face the Washington Senators lefty,

Chuck Stobbs. With two outs and one man on base, New York was ahead 2-1. Hank Bauer and I were crouched on one knee in the nearby on-deck circle.

The first pitch from Stobbs was called a ball by the plate umpire, Jim Honochick. Stobbs wound up, took a quick look at the base runner, and delivered his second pitch, a chest-high fast ball. Seeing Mantle's mighty swing and hearing the ball crush against the bat, left little doubt he had hit a home run. I expected Mantle's well-hit ball to land somewhere in the stadium's left-field bleachers, as I had seen three or four times before during the Yankees' two days of batting practice. Not this time. It was as if time was standing still. The ball just kept going and going, higher and higher. It appeared to glance off the fifty-six foot "Mr. Boh" (beer ad) sign in the bleachers as it sailed totally out of the stadium.

This tremendous home run by Mickey Mantle was the first ball ever to clear Griffith Stadium's left-field bleachers since they were built in 1924. Ruth didn't do it, nor did any of those other powerhouses in years before. Mickey Mantle's homer was calculated to have traveled 565 feet, and it became known as the "tape-measure" home run.

Mr. October

To get my juices flowing, a friend of mine—with World Series tickets— invited me to join him at Yankee Stadium for Game 6 of the 1977 World Series. I'd lived in New York for three years. This would not be my first trip to "The House that Ruth Built." I had made this trek at least four times before, but tonight, Tuesday, October 18, 1977, was special. It was my first World Series game, and the Yankees were facing the tough National League champs, the Los Angeles Dodgers. As Game 6 got underway, the Yankees were up three games to two over the Dodgers.

As my friend and I took our seats, we talked briefly about an ongoing rumor being hyped by the sports media. Seems that Yankees manager Billy Martin had accused Reggie Jackson of loafing on a ball that was hit into short right field during a June 18th game against the Boston Red Sox. Martin, known to have a short temper, had pulled both his pitcher and Jackson, and replaced Jackson with Paul Blair in the sixth inning of what would end up a 10-4 thrashing by the Red Sox.

Had the conflict between Martin and Jackson passed, or would it resurface? We mused over the question, then got down to the serious stuff—getting ready to watch the ballgame.

Looking back, little attention focused on Jackson's first at-bat when he was walked on four straight pitches by Dodger pitcher Burt Hooton. As the game moved along, Jackson again came to bat against Hooton in the bottom of the fourth inning, with the Yankees trailing 3-2. With Thurman Munson on first, Jackson hammered Hooton's first pitch for a home run, sending the Yankees ahead with a 4-3 lead; knocking Hooton out of the game.

An inning later—in the bottom of the fifth—Jackson reappeared against relief pitcher Elias Sosa. On his first swing, Jackson sent the ball into the bleachers—chalking up an impressive two home runs on two swings.

As Jackson—the first batter up in the bottom of the eighth—stepped into the batter's box to face knuckleballer, Charlie Hough, fans went wild chanting Reg-GIE! Reg-GIE! Reg-GIE! The cheers echoed through the stadium so loudly that we could barely carry on a conversation without having to shout. Then it happened! On the first pitch, Jackson electrified the crowd of 56,407 with his third home run into the center-field bleachers. With that historic blast, Jackson had now belted three homers on three consecutive first pitches thrown by three different pitchers. Those three home runs in a single World Series game tied Babe Ruth's record (Ruth accomplished this twice; once in 1926 and again in 1928).

When the reporters later compared Jackson's blasts to Ruth's feat, Jackson responded, "Babe Ruth was great. I'm just lucky." (Albert Pujols (Game 3, 2011) and Pablo Sandoval (Game 1, 2012) would later join Ruth and Jackson as the only players in history to hit three home runs in a single World Series game.)

Reggie Jackson "Mr. October" also set the mark in 1977 for the most homers hit in a World Series with five.

On January 5, 1993, "Mr. October" was elected to the Baseball Hall of Fame.

The Mazeroski Moment—October 13, 1960, Pittsburgh's Forbes Field

In the winner-take-all showdown Game 7 of the 1960 World Series, some 36,680 fans crammed the stands as the final game between the New York Yankees and Pittsburgh Pirates began.

Having already won seven of the past eleven World Series, the New York Yankees were heavily favored, especially since they had already won three games in this Series with blowout scores of 16-3, 10-0 and 12-0. The Pirates had won the three lower scoring (6-4, 3-2, and 5-2) games, and they hadn't won a single World Series championship since 1925.

Game on: Vernon Law started for the Pirates as he had beaten the Yankees in two previous games. Manager Casey Stengel[1], gave Bob Turley the nod to take the pitcher's mound for the Yankees.

As the game progressed, the lead shifted three times before the Yankees rallied with two runs to tie the game at 9-9 in the top of the ninth inning. Once the Yankees were retired, their fifth reliever, Ralph Terry, returned to the mound in the bottom of the ninth. His job was to not allow the Pirates to score a run, so the Yankees could bat again in the top of the tenth inning.

The first batter to step up to the plate was Bill Mazeroski, or "Maz," as he was affectionately called by local fans. Terry's first pitch was a fastball down the middle, but high. Ball one. The crowd's anxiety built as Terry went into his windup and delivered a slider that moved right over the plate. "Maz", never known as a power hitter, unleashed his bat and solidly connected. An enormous blast! The crowd began screaming wildly—could it be...could it be...ah, yes! The Yankees left fielder, Berra, turned around to chase the ball, but it was all in vain. The ball flew over the 18-foot high wall and disappeared as it passed beyond the 406 marker. Game over.

As Mazeroski rounded the bases, waving his batting helmet over his head in jubilation, Ralph Terry walked silently off the mound, headed for the dugout. New York's remaining players simply stood and watched in stunned disbelief. The Pirates had pulled off the nearly

impossible: They were outscored, outhit, and outplayed, but still managed to pull out a victory.

With that mammoth "walk-off" home run blast off the bat of Bill Mazeroski, the Pittsburgh Pirates won the 1960 World Series championship. Years later, Mickey Mantle was quoted as saying that losing the 1960 Series was the biggest disappointment of his career. For Bill Mazeroski, it was the highlight. Although only one official error was recorded, Yogi Berra said, the Yankees had "made too many wrong mistakes."

Game 7's final stats showed that the lead had shifted between the two teams four times. In total, the two teams had compiled 19 runs, and 24 hits, without a single strikeout. Equally astounding was the length of this high scoring game: 2 hours and 36 minutes—the shortest game in World Series history.

The Impossible Has Happened!

Let's travel back in time to Dodger Stadium in Los Angeles, California, and arrive there on October 15, 1988: It's Game 1 of the World Series; the National League's champion, L.A. Dodgers against the American League champs, the Oakland Athletics (A's).

Unfortunately, during the National League playoffs, Kirk Gibson, star player for the L.A. Dodgers, suffered injuries to both legs. Also ill with a stomach virus, he was not expected to play.

With the Dodgers at-bat in the bottom half of the first inning, Mickey Hatcher hit a two-run homer and Los Angeles took an early lead. In the next inning, Jose Canseco hit a grand slam homer, making the score 4-2 in Oakland's favor. In the bottom of the sixth inning, the Dodgers scored a run, cutting Oakland's lead to just one run. The Dodgers retired the A's in the top of the ninth.

Going into the Dodgers' final at-bat in the bottom of the ninth, Oakland's closer Dennis Eckersley— baseball's best closer with 45 saves—was brought in to pitch and seal the win for Oakland. Facing the bottom of the batting order, Eckersley retired the first two batters, and then walked pinch hitter Mike Davis, a power hitter. Dave Anderson, who had been waiting in the on-deck circle to pinch hit for the pitcher, abruptly turned and headed back to the dugout. (Manager Lasorda would later reveal that he sent weak-hitting Dave Anderson to the on-deck circle as a ploy. He said, "I figured Eckersley would pitch more carefully to Davis with the right-hander on deck. If he'd seen Gibson on deck, he would have pitched Davis differently.")

To the great surprise of everyone—fans, announcers, and Oakland's ballplayers—Kirk Gibson hobbled from the dugout and took his place in the batter's box. Once a 2-2 count was reached on Gibson, Davis stole second. Now with two outs, Gibson worked his way to a 3-2 count. With everyone in the stadium frozen—Eckersley threw his next pitch. Gibson, using nothing but his wrists, took an awkward swing, but connected solidly, and the ball rocketed off his bat and sailed over the right-field fence bringing the Dodgers a miraculous 5-4 win. With Gibson limping around each of the bases and pumping his fist, his ecstatic teammates stormed the field and the celebration began.

According to NBC broadcaster Vin Scully, *the impossible just happened!* The L. A. Dodgers won the game, 5–4. Gibson would not have another appearance in that World Series. The Dodgers went on to defeat the Oakland A's in the World Series, four games to one.

Ultimate Sports' Fantasy, October 23, 1993

This story takes us back to Game 6 of the 1993 World Series between the Toronto Blue Jays and Philadelphia Phillies, being played at Toronto's Skydome. The Blue Jays, vying for their second straight World Series championship, held the lead in this Fall Classic, three games to two, but were in serious trouble, thanks to the Phillies' five-run seventh inning that included Lenny Dykstra's three-run homer. (Dykstra, having a great post-season for the Phillies, had already hit nine home runs, scored eight times and driven in five runs in this World Series.)

As they moved into the bottom of the ninth, with the Blue Jays trailing the Phillies 6-5, the Phillies and their fans had hopes and visions of a Game 7. The Phillies manager ordered a pitching change. Relief pitcher, Mitch "Wild Thing" Williams came in to secure the final three outs that would send the Series into a Game 7 final. Williams didn't just inherit his "Wild Thing" nickname; he was known to be wild, whether "on" or not. So no one was surprised when he walked the Blue Jays' leadoff batter Rickey Henderson on four straight pitches to open the bottom of the ninth. With one on base, Williams threw nine pitches to Devon White before White flied out to left field; Henderson, played it safe, and remained on first base. Paul Molitor, designated hitter for the Jays, stepped up to the plate. Molitor, who had previously tripled and hit a homer in this game—was batting close to .500 in this Series. After working the count to 1-1, Molitor drilled the next pitch to center field for a single. Henderson held up at second base.

With runners on first and second and one out, Joe Carter stepped into the batter's box. Philly fans, on their feet began chanting, "wild thing, wild thing…double-play." They knew that a double play would end the game with a Phillies win, and send the Series into a final, winner-take-all, Game 7. Blue Jays fans not to be outdone, began standing, clapping in synch, and shouting in hopes that a single would bring home the runner from second base, making it a tie game, and keeping the opportunity alive for a Jays win and possible championship. Williams' first two pitches to Carter were called balls with both out of the strike zone.

Working his way back to a 2-2 count, Williams delivered his next pitch. As the ball reached the plate, Carter took a powerful swing and connected solidly. The ball exploded like a bomb off his bat, and traveled towards the foul pole mounted at the left-field stands. Those who watched appeared mesmerized, possibly thinking…foul or fair? Carter, as he sprinted towards first-base, followed the flight of the ball, perhaps wondering the same…fair or foul ball? All doubt faded as the ball disappeared over the left-field wall in fair territory.

The Blue Jays had turned what looked like a probable Game 6 loss into an 8-6 win and a World Series victory.

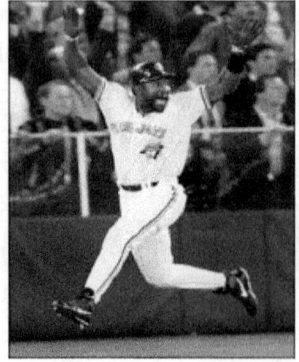

Joe Carter later said, "I actually dreamed of that moment many times. I dreamed of that moment when I was a little kid. I'd be sitting at my father's garage and daydreaming about that moment. I even wrote it down a few times: My dream is to hit a home run to win the World Series." It was the ultimate sports fantasy.

CHAPTER TWO

What Are The Odds?

"I'll be home soon, Ma. The pitchers are starting to curve me."

—Unknown Rookie

Anytime a rookie makes it to the big leagues it is difficult, and even harder is that moment when he steps into the batter's box for the first time. If he is playing at home, there will be cheers; if away on the road—all he will hear are boos and little else. He is possibly thinking something like, "I made it to The Show. I'm here and I must not fail."

The rookie, taking his place in the batter's box for the first time, palms sweaty, his heart racing as fast as Aroldis Chapman's 100 mph fastball, watches intently as the pitcher stares down at him and goes into his windup—the pitch is on its way. *"Just a hit, anything, but don't strike out."* The furthest thing from the rookie's mind is hitting a home run on his first at-bat. He knows the odds of doing this are minuscule, if not impossible. Even superstars like Babe Ruth, Ted Williams, Mickey Mantle, Hank Aaron, and numerous others didn't make that happen. As the ball reaches the plate, the rookie takes a big cut; the ball meets the bat solidly, in the middle. It rockets off the bat, sailing well into the stands for a home run. Exciting? You better believe it!

According to the record books, similar scenarios have taken place only 114 times. Of those 114 rookie home runs hit first time at-bat, 29 of them were hit off the first pitch thrown. Nineteen of those rookies never hit another home run during their entire major league careers.

Four of those home runs were grand-slams. Bill Duggleby of the Philadelphia Phillies made the record books on April 21, 1898, with the first ever grand-slam home run during a player's first time at-bat. It took another hundred and seven years for a player to duplicate that feat!

Not until August 31, 2005, when rookie pinch-hitter Jeremy Hermida of the Florida Marlins stepped up to his first time at-bat would baseball fans be treated to such a spectacular play again. The bases were loaded and St. Louis Cardinals pitcher Al Reyes was on the mound. The crack of Hermida's bat hitting the ball sounded throughout the park as he slammed the ball into right field for a clean sweep—four runs for the Marlins.

Defying the Odds:

So what about the other two first time at-bat grand-slam home runs? Every once in a while, even in baseball, the stars align. When they do, extraordinary things happen. As if by magic, phenomena occur that are almost beyond belief. For Kevin Kouzmanoff, a Triple-A ballplayer for Buffalo in the Cleveland Indians' organization, his mojo came to life with an early morning phone call on Saturday, September 2, 2006.

Good news! It was the call that every minor leaguer dreams of and prays for. He was being called up to "The Show" to substitute for the Indians' injured designated hitter that evening in a game against the Texas Rangers. He had to catch the next plane to Dallas.

Naturally, such exciting news brought about a little anxiety, but upon arrival at the airport, Kouzmanoff's uneasiness rapidly shifted into a high-gear stage of nervousness—his plane to Dallas was delayed. Running late and finally arriving at the Rangers' ballpark in Arlington, Kevin encountered another bump-in-the-road: He couldn't locate the visiting team's clubhouse, and discovered it took some time to find someone who could direct him. Once inside the locker room and into his uniform—still rushing, he barely makes it to the dugout in time for batting practice.

What a wonderful, but incredibly stressful day, Kouzmanoff thought. It had all started with that phone call. He made it, but it had been a nerve-racking day. He hoped this is not an omen sign of things to come.

Inside the dugout, the manager informed Kouzmanoff that, as the designated hitter, he would be batting seventh in the lineup. *Ah seventh*, he thought. This meant an inning or two to relax and calm down from all that rushing. Not to be! The Indians' bats got hot in the top of the first inning. In no time the bases were loaded, and batter number seven was next up. Kouzmanoff left the on-deck circle, and stepped up to the plate. As he had done in the minors, he took his stance, dug-in with his cleats, and tapped the plate a couple of times. Looking up he saw Edinson Volquez, staring down at him from the pitcher's mound. Volquez went into his stretch, taking a quick glance at the runner on third, and fired.

As he had done so many times before, Kouzmanoff focused on the ball as it approached the plate, and took a powerful swing and connected. Connected on the first pitch ever thrown to him in a major league game. Unbelievable! Feeling the impact as the ball met his bat, Kevin looked up in time to see what reminded him of a "rocket" shooting over the center field wall. Grand-slam home run! Score: Indians 5, Rangers 0.

It would be Kouzmanoff's only hit in this game, going 1-for-4. After Cleveland's 6-5 victory over the Rangers, Kevin Kouzmanoff was quoted as saying, "I don't even remember running around the bases. I couldn't believe I did it. I still can't believe I did it."

Oftentimes, we overlook stories that can be much more interesting than what happened during any particular ballgame. Kevin Kouzmanoff's is such a story.

Another is an incredible story that could be titled, the *Ultimate Underdog*. It's about a small, yet tenacious kid who loved baseball, and refused to surrender to claims that he wasn't talented or big enough to play the game. When Daniel Nava started high school, he weighed 70 pounds soaking wet. He could barely hit the ball out of the infield, but he kept practicing: shagging fly balls, throwing balls from the outfield to various bases, taking numerous cuts in the batting cage, running laps, and doing strength exercises. All his work was paying off. Nava was not only developing into a better ballplayer, he was also getting bigger and stronger.

Nava thought he was ready, so he tried out for college baseball, but failed to make the team. Due to financial problems, Nava had to transfer to a less expensive junior college. There he showed he could play baseball with the best of them. Nava batted over .400 in two seasons. With that record, Nava returned to his old college on a full scholarship. This time, he would not to be denied. He not only made his college's team, he led the West Coast Conference in hitting, without making an error.

Still, Daniel couldn't attract the attention of any major league scouts. Dejected, he chose to play for the Chico Outlaws of the independent Golden League. Shortly after he joined the Outlaws, Daniel was cut from the team, only to return later that season to replace an outfielder who left.

It was at this point that Nava's perseverance paid off. David Kaval, president of the now-defunct Golden League, saw talent in Daniel Nava where others had failed to notice. Kaval, a close friend of Jared Porter, assistant director of Red Sox scouting, told Porter about Nava, and convinced him to take a close look at the young player. He did and the Sox were impressed.

On October 20, 2007, the Boston Red Sox paid the Chico Outlaws $1.00 (That's right. It takes "good and valuable consideration" even if it's only $1.00

for a contract to be valid.) for the rights to sign Nava. Starting off in Class A ball in the minor leagues, Nava quickly worked his way up to the Sox's Triple-A team, Pawtucket. He was hitting .294 with 8 home runs, and had knocked in 38 runs when he, like Kouzmanoff, received that phone call every minor leaguer waits and prays for—to report immediately to the Boston Red Sox. That Saturday morning call on June 12, 2010, like Kevin Kouzmanoff's call, had been triggered by an injury to a first-string player.

By luck, Nava's parents had been in Indianapolis watching their son play for Pawtucket, and were in the process of packing for their trip home to California. After learning that their son was going to play in that afternoon's interleague game between the Boston Red Sox and Philadelphia Phillies at Fenway Park, his parents quickly changed their plans and headed to Boston. A travel delay caused them to arrive late at Fenway. As the two rushed to their seats their son trotted towards his position in left field.

Neither team scored in the first inning, but in the top of the 2nd, the Phillies scored two runs before being retired. With Boston at-bat in the bottom of the 2nd, the first batter up (Drew) hit a home run. Two singles followed. Nava, the ninth batter, passed the Red Sox manager, Terry Francona, on his way to the on-deck circle. "I wonder where my folks are sitting." Nava said. Francona replied, "I don't care. Go get a hit."

As Nava took his place in the on-deck circle, batter number eight ripped another single to load the bases. With no outs and the bases loaded, Nava stepped up to the plate, in his first major league appearance. On the mound, Joe Blanton was pitching for the Phillies. Blanton glanced at the runner on third as he went into his stretch, and delivered what appeared to be a fastball over the plate. Nava, a switch-hitter, batting from the left side of the plate, swung the bat with all his might. The explosive sound that resonated from the contact of the ball meeting the bat left little doubt, this was a home run. The ball flew directly into the Red Sox bullpen in right-center field.

Grand slam! With that solo blast, rookie Daniel Nava of the Boston Red Sox hit a grand slam at his first at-bat on the first pitch. When asked about his potential folk-hero status, Nava said "It's one game. We all know that. It's one game. There's still tomorrow, and who knows what's going to happen tomorrow? You can go from having a good at-bat, to the next at-bat, looking like you've sometimes never played baseball. Obviously, I'm enjoying it right now. The road I've taken hasn't been a road with a lot of flashing lights and what not."

Kouzmanoff and Nava are the only players to ever hit a grand slam home run on the first pitch of their major league careers.

Inside-the-park dinger

In baseball jargon, the definition of an inside-the-park dinger is when the batter hits a home run without having the ball leave the field of play.

While serving as a major league batboy during the early '50s, I had always wanted to witness an inside-the-park dinger. I have seen no-hitters, unbelievable catches both in the infield and outfield, and witnessed spectacular home runs such as Mickey Mantle's "tape-measure" one he hit out of Griffith Stadium in 1953. I have also watched from just outside of home plate as a triple play was executed. In spite of all of those fantastic plays, I never got to personally witness the thing I most longed to see; the rare feat of a speedy batter tearing round the bases and safely crossing home plate ahead of a fielder's throw—to achieve an inside-the-park dinger or home run.

My wish came true as I was working on this book, even though I only saw it on TV. Here's what happened:

Shortly after turning on the television to watch the New York Mets play the Kansas City Royals in Game 1 of the 2015 World Series at Kauffman Stadium, the home of the Royals, I watched as the Mets failed to get a hit in the top half of the first. It was now the Royals turn at-bat in the bottom-half of that inning. While not yet settled in to watch the game, I was only half-heartily focusing on the Mets' pitcher, Matt Harvey, as he took his wind-up and threw his first pitch to the Royals' lead-off batter, Alcides Escobar. Escobar smashed that first pitch—an over the plate fastball—into the gap in deep left-center field. After what appeared to be some miscommunication between outfielders Yoenis Cespedes and Michael Conforto, the centerfielder, Cespedes, appeared to misjudge the ball in what should have been an out. He then attempted to make an awkward backhanded stab at the ball while on the run—but missed; the ball bounced towards the wall. By the time the Mets were able to retrieve the ball, Escobar was rounding third. I was surprised to learn that no error was charged to Cespedes. To me, this ball should have been caught. Oh well, I am not the official scorer. Since no error was called on the play, Escobar was credited for hitting the first World Series inside-the-park homer since Mule Haas did it for the Philadelphia A's in 1929. Escobar's dinger was only the twelfth in World Series history and just the second first-pitch homer in Series annals. The other belongs to the Yankees' Derek Jeter; Game 4 in 2000 against the Mets.

(Escobar's World Series ball was retrieved and authenticated by Major League Baseball with a QR code and a hologram. It was sold at auction for $19,200.) Check out the action: http://m.mlb.com/news/article/155717014/alcides-escobar-hits-inside-the-park-home-run.

Major League Baseball's rules require that for an inside-the-park home run to be confirmed as such, the batter must touch all four bases (first, second, third, and safely cross home plate) without a fielder from the opposition tagging him out. (If the defensive team commits an error during this play, it is not statistically scored as a home run, but rather as advancement on an error.) An inside-the-park dinger or home run is treated the same as a regular home run in the player's season and career totals.

An inside-the-park home run is extremely rare today, and Escobar's homer on the first pitch of the first game of a World Series is one to be remembered. In decades past, it was not uncommon to see such a feat take place. For example, Jesse Burkett (playing 1890-1905) holds the record for career inside-the-park home runs with fifty-five. Tommy Leach (1898-1918) owns second place, with forty-eight, and the legendary Ty Cobb (1905-1928) of the Dead Ball Era's Detroit Tigers is locked in third with forty-six inside-the-park dingers.

Much smaller stadiums, cautious managers, and less daring base-runners have turned the inside-the-park dinger into a rarity in this modern era. Today, as witnessed by Escobar's homer, this amazing feat has become increasingly extraordinary, and is typically accomplished only by a fast base runner hitting the ball in such a way that the ball bounces some distance away from the opposing team's fielders.

In 1966, Richie Allen of the Phillies and Sonny Jackson of the Astros each hit three inside-the-park dingers, and in 1958 Mickey Mantle hit three for the Yankees. In 1979, of the six total home runs that Willie Wilson hit—five were inside-the-park dingers, a total that has not been achieved since.

Among active players, Jimmy Rollins recently traded (December 2014) to the Los Angeles Dodgers by the Philadelphia Phillies, currently leads the majors with four inside-the-park dingers; only 51 shy of catching the legendary Jesse Burkett, who played from 1890-1905.

During the recent post-war era, outfielder Willie Wilson—who played most of his career with the Kansas City Royals—is the modern day leader for inside-the-park dingers. Wilson hit a total of 12 during his 19-year career.

First At-bat Dingers

Getting any type of hit—single, double, triple or home run—on a player's first time at-bat in the majors is something special. Hitting an inside-the-park-dinger on the first time at-bat, that's a memory that will never fade.

Only two players have gone down in baseball history for hitting an inside-the-park dinger on their first time at-bat in the major leagues. Luke Stuart did it in 1921 and Johnnie LeMaster accomplished his feat in 1975. *Who are these two guys?*

Luke Stuart was 29 when he broke into the big leagues on July 28, 1921 with the St. Louis Browns. On August 8, 1921, he stepped into the batter's box in the ninth inning facing the Washington Senators' premier pitcher, Walter Johnson. Stuart's well-placed hit combined with his lightening speed resulted in an inside-the-park dinger that brought in two runs. *(This author was unable to confirm Stuart's home run was a dinger, as no distinction was made in 1921 as to type of home run.)*

In the mid-1990s, the *Complete Baseball Record Book* published by *The Sporting News* recognized Stuart as the first American League player to hit a home run in his first major league at-bat.

No wonder only a few people have heard of Luke Stuart, the 1921 MLB rookie. His major league career ended after only three games with the St. Louis Browns.

On September 2, 1975, Johnnie LeMaster, San Francisco Giants, hit an inside-the-park home run in his first at-bat against the L.A. Dodgers during the Giants' 7-3 win.

In the 1970s, Candlestick Park had artificial turf. LeMaster was quoted as saying, "Don Sutton was pitching. The first pitch he throws me was a big curve and I had no chance of hitting it. Some fan in the stands yells, 'Hey kid, this is the big leagues!' The next pitch was the same, and I swung and missed again. The same fan yells out the same thing, and I'm thinking to myself, no kidding, I've never seen a pitch like that! But, the next pitch was a fast ball and I hit a line drive up the middle. It hit a [artificial turf] seam on the field and the ball jumped over the center fielder's head. I started running like crazy and I got a standup inside-the-park home run."

Johnnie LeMaster played for four teams during his twelve major league seasons—ten with the San Francisco Giants—but hit only 22 home runs during his 3,191 times at-bat.

One More Oddity

Hank Aaron, Barry Bonds, and Babe Ruth, all hit career home run number 700 during the same inning. Aaron hit his on July 21, 1973, in the third inning off of Phillies pitcher Ken Brett; Bonds connected on September 17, 2004, in the third inning off of Padres pitcher Jake Peavy; and Babe Ruth hit his 700th homer on July 13, 1934, in the third inning off of Tigers pitcher Tommy Bridges.

CHAPTER THREE

Head Down, Spikes Flying

"Thou shalt not steal. I mean defensively. On offense, indeed thou shall steal and thou must."

—*Branch Rickey, baseball executive*

Spectacular home runs make the game exciting. But there's so much more to the thrill of baseball than some power hitter connecting and sending the ball out of the park. If it's excitement at every level of the game that you are looking for, we can't ignore what takes place on the base-paths.

The First Stolen Base

In the blink of an eye, the speedster takes advantage of an almost imperceptible hesitation by the pitcher, and is off towards the next base. A stolen base generally occurs when a base runner successfully advances to the next base without the benefit of a batter hitting the ball. Successful base stealing requires the base runner to be fast and possess good instincts and timing.

Legend has it that Ned Cuthbert, playing for the Philadelphia Keystones, stole the first base in 1863. He ran from first to second base without the benefit of a batted ball and the umpire determined that there was no rule forbidding this maneuver.

Cuthbert's safe steal opened the floodgates, and more and more teams took advantage of the game's poorly defined base running rules. By 1887, base-stealing had gotten out of hand. Six major league players stole over 100 bases each, and seven teams recorded a minimum of 350 stolen bases that year. Two of the seven, the St. Louis Cardinals and the Cincinnati Red Stockings each exceeded 500 stolen bases. This free-for-all in taking advantage of vague criterion forced a few base-running rule changes be implemented. Those changes included requiring base runners to touch each base when running on the base paths; base runner to be out if hit by a batted ball; stolen bases no longer credited when a base runner reached an extra base on a base hit from another player; player is out once he has acquired legal possession of a base, and runs the bases in reverse order for the purpose of confusing the defense or making a travesty of the game.

As organized baseball moved into the early 1900s—the period that became known as the Dead-Ball Era—teams began to strategically plan both their offensive and defensive actions. This new form of team-planning strategies revolved around what became known as a "small ball" style of play—a strategy that focused on getting batters on base. Once batters were on base, the challenge was to advance them into scoring positions through the use of walks, sacrifice bunts or fly balls, hit-and-run plays, and stealing bases.

Speed dominated power—home runs were rare. For example, in 1913, Frank "Home Run" Baker, hit a grand total of only 12 home runs to lead the American League and won that year's batting title. Baker would go on to lead the American League in home runs for four consecutive seasons; hitting eleven in 1911, ten in 1912, twelve in 1913, and only nine homers in 1914. (Power hitting, or swinging for the fences, rarely happened until Babe Ruth gave up taking his occasional turns at pitching—with its limited plate appearances and switching to playing the outfield and batting on a full-time basis. With that change, Ruth started slugging the ball out of the park with much more frequency.)

Strategic "small ball" play dominated the game throughout the Dead-Ball Era, and as base stealing grew in popularity, two scrappy and aggressive speedsters, Ty Cobb and Clyde Milan, thrilled fans as they exhibited their skills, speed, and tenacity on the base paths. Each of these greats stole close to 100 bases in a single season. In Ty Cobb's 24-year career, he would steal a staggering total of 892 bases.

While the Dead-Ball Era is estimated to have spanned the years between 1901 and 1920, the actual time and reasons for its sudden demise, are arguable. While many of those base-running rules and strategies in place during those earlier times have been improved and refined, and continues to excite today's modern fans. As with any fast-moving sports strategy, a few weird moments add color to the many well executed maneuvers, as in this story told by Tigers' outfielder Davy Jones about his teammate, Jimmy St. Vrain:

The Third-Base Saga

"He [Jimmy St. Vrain] was a left-handed pitcher and a right-handed batter. But an absolutely terrible hitter—never even got a loud foul off anybody. *(Note the photo shows Jimmy posing with a baseball bat in hand, even though he was a very poor hitter.)*

Well, one day [May 30, 1902] we were playing the Pittsburgh Pirates and Jimmy was pitching for us. The first two times he went up to bat that day he looked simply awful. So when he came back after striking out the second time, Frank Selee, our manager, said, 'Jimmy, you're a left-handed pitcher, why don't you turn around and bat from the left side, too? Why not try it?'

Actually, Frank was half-kidding, but Jimmy took him seriously. So the next time he went up he batted left-handed. Turned around and stood on the opposite side of the plate from where he was used to, you know. And darned if he didn't actually hit the ball. He tapped a slow roller down to Honus Wagner at shortstop and took off as fast as he could go…but instead of running to first base, he headed for *third!*

Oh, my God! What bedlam! Everybody yelling and screaming at poor Jimmy as he raced to third base; head down, spikes flying, determined to get there ahead of the throw. Later on, Honus told us that as a matter of fact, he almost *did* throw the ball to third. 'I'm standing there with the ball in my hand,' Honus said, 'looking at this guy running from home to third, and for an instant there I swear I didn't know *where* to throw the damn ball. And when I finally *did throw* to first, I wasn't at all sure it was the right thing to do!'

Jones further commented that "St. Vrain was disoriented by hitting from an unfamiliar spot, and then dashed for third rather than first, much to the amusement of Wagner and the other Pirates. When later asked for an explanation, all Jimmy could say was, 'Well, I always was used to run[ning] the way my bat pointed.'"

While the veracity of this story is questionable[2], St. Vrain's propensity for executing weird maneuvers is supported by the following story that appeared in the *San Diego Union* newspaper on March 30, 1930:

"According to Jimmy St. Vrain's former manager, Mike Fisher, while St. Vrain was playing for the Portland Giants of the Pacific Coast League in 1904, and during a game against the Tacoma Tigers, St. Vrain, positioned as a runner on second base, inexplicably reached out and snared a Tacoma line drive headed for the outfield, turning an RBI base hit into the third out. When confronted back in the dugout, St. Vrain allegedly told Fisher that he didn't know why he did it."

One thing that appears true is that Jimmy St. Vrain was a very poor hitter. His MLB batting average 0.97.

When Bizarre Equals Bizarre

On April 19, 2013, the Milwaukee Brewers played the Chicago Cubs at home. The Brewers' second-year shortstop, Jean Segura, hit a single in the bottom of the eighth inning. He stole second base, returned to first base during a bizarre rundown, and was tagged out trying to steal second base again. Veteran umpire Tom Hallion ruled that Segura "technically stole second, stole first, then got thrown out stealing second."

Here's what actually happened: After Segura successfully stole second, Ryan Braun walked; men are now on first and second. With the Brewers cleanup hitter up, Segura got caught off second base—trapped in a rundown between second and third—by the Cubs pitcher, Shawn Camp. At the same time, and almost in unison, Braun took off for second, as Segura returned to that very same base. With two men now on second, the umpire called Braun out. At the moment of the umpire's call, the play should have ended. However, Segura, who had slid headfirst into second got up and started trotting towards the Brewers' dugout near first base thinking he was out. As the confusion commenced to unravel, Segura promptly ran to first base and stood on the bag; he was then held there by that base's coach.

Is it legal for a base runner to proceed in the opposite direction?

The umpire citing Rule 7.08(i)[3] declared that Segura was safe once he occupied first base. On the next pitch, Segura attempted to steal second again, but this time he was thrown out by the catcher to retire the side.

Bad to Worse

June 27, 1986 had to be one of the most embarrassing days ever for rookie Robby Thompson of the San Francisco Giants. He was caught stealing bases a record-setting four times in a single game. Thompson's only crutch to help relieve some of his embarrassment was that this game against the Cincinnati Reds lasted twelve innings.

Here's what happened: The Giants were in front by a score of 5-1. With two outs, Thompson hit a single in the fourth inning with no one on base. Safe on first, Thompson suddenly took off in an attempt to steal second base; it didn't work. He was thrown out by Cincinnati's catcher, Bo Diaz, to retire the side. Thompson came up again in the sixth inning and smacked an RBI single to give the Giants a 6-2 lead. Once again, Thompson challenged Diaz's throwing ability. He was called out at second base; ending the inning. By the time this game reached the ninth inning, Cincinnati had stormed back, and the game was tied 6-6. Thompson led off the top of the ninth by lining a single to center but was again thrown out in his attempt to steal second.

As the game moved into extra innings, Thompson stepped up to the plate in the top of the eleventh with two outs. He went down swinging on his third strike. Diaz failed to hold onto the ball and this error allowed Thompson to reach first base safely. With Thompson on first base, the Cincinnati pitcher went into his stretch, then made a quick throw to first—catching Thompson off the base; a rundown. Thompson was again tagged out. Officially, this out was recorded as an attempt to steal second.

Thompson went into the MLB record books for the most times (four) caught attempting to steal in a single game. The Giants won the game 7-6 in twelve innings.

Who Sez You Can't Steal First?

Germany Schaefer may well be regarded as the "father" of all baseball clowns as result of his antics, acts of clowning, and showmanship on the ball field during the early 1900s. While baseball fans were delighted and entertained wherever he played, it was not Schaefer's talent as a ballplayer, nor his clown acts or showmanship that gained him his greatest recognition. No, it was for *stealing first base*, a strategy that forced a baseball rule change.

On August 4, 1911, in a game between the Washington Senators and Chicago White Sox, in the bottom of the ninth inning, Germany Schaefer was on first base and Clyde Milan on third. With what would be the winning run if Milan scored, Schaefer suddenly took off towards second base—in a clever attempt to draw a throw to second that would give Milan the opportunity to score the winning run. However, the Chicago White Sox catcher, Fred Payne, did not fall for this astute maneuver. He allowed the base to be stolen by not making the throw to second.

Safely on second, Schaefer took his lead off the bag on the first base side. On the next pitch, he promptly stole first, and the White Sox manager Hugh Duffy, came out of the dugout to argue. With this distraction, Schaefer again took off for second base—this time he got caught in a rundown. Milan attempted to steal home, but was tagged out to end the inning.

The umpire, Tom Connolly, insisted that Schaefer's stealing of first base was legal as no rule prevented such a maneuver[4]. The MLB rule to prevent stealing bases in reverse order was adopted in 1920.

One Great Succeeded...One Failed!

In the 1926 World Series, the great Babe Ruth made what many perceived as a crucial and unbelievable base-running error.

On October 10, 1926, a cold and damp day in New York City, a crowd of 38,093 die-hard baseball fans settled into their seats at Yankee Stadium to watch the New York Yankees take on the St. Louis Cardinals, in what would be the seventh and deciding game of the 1926 World Series. In the bottom of the seventh inning with St. Louis leading 3-2, the Cardinals' relief pitcher, Grover Cleveland Alexander was sent in to stifle a threatening New York rally. He did. When the game worked its way to the bottom of the ninth inning— the Yankees final time at-bat—Alexander was still on the mound, trying to protect the 3-2 Cardinals lead for the World Series championship.

With Alexander facing the top of the Yankees batting order, the first two batters (Combs and Koenig) both grounded out to third base. Now with two outs in the bottom of the ninth—in this do or die inning—Babe Ruth came to the plate. Up to this point, Ruth's performance in this Series had been outstanding. He had six hits for twenty times at-bat, including four home runs. Ruth had also walked ten of those twenty times. Since Ruth represented the game-tying run, many believed that Alexander would walk Ruth again. However, Alexander decided to cautiously pitch to Ruth, and worked the count to a full three and two. The next pitch was a curve outside, and Ruth, for the fourth time in this game, took first base on a walk.

The next batter, Bob Meusel, stepped into the batter's box. On the first pitch (some sources say it was the second pitch), Ruth hesitated momentarily—then took off running for second on a delayed steal. Meusel swung at the pitch and missed; the Cardinals' catcher, O'Farrell, threw a rifle shot to Hornsby, who tagged Ruth out. At that moment, the game ended, and the Cardinals headed home with the World Series championship.

Babe Ruth, although his overall performance during that seven-game World Series was spectacular, was blamed for the loss of the Series championship.

Move that 1926 clock forward thirty-four years to the 1960 World Series. It's October 13, 1960 and the New York Yankees and the Pittsburgh Pirates are tied at three games each going into this seventh and deciding game at Pittsburgh's Forbes Field. At the top of the ninth, the Yankees are behind 9-8.

With one out, Mickey Mantle on first and Gil McDougald on third, Yogi Berra hits a sharp grounder to first baseman Rocky Nelson, who quickly steps on first for the second out. Mantle, already with a good lead off first, turned and dove back into first, avoiding the tag and distracting Nelson. This quick maneuver allowed McDougald to score the tying run. (Over the years, those analyzing this play appear to have reached a consensus that all this happened so fast, that Mantle's quick maneuver must have been instinctive.)

Hero and Goat—One Misstep and Everything Changes

Back to the comparison of Babe Ruth and Mickey Mantle on the base-path: With the World Series at stake, Ruth ran to second, Mantle retreated to first. In each case, the opposite was expected. Each of their decisions was sound. The decisive difference was the result: Mantle succeeded, Ruth failed. In a results-driven sport, Mantle was congratulated and Ruth criticized. Had the Pirates' Rocky Nelson, been a little more alert and Cardinals catcher, Bob O'Farrell, a little less, Mantle would have been labeled a goat for a bonehead decision to head back to first, and Ruth commended for a savvy steal.

Triple Steal...Twice

On July 25, 1930, the Philadelphia Athletics pulled off a triple steal *twice* during the same game against the Cleveland Indians. This was the first and only time in Major League Baseball history that such an event has taken place.

The A's first triple steal took place in the first inning and involved Al Simmons, Bing Miller, and Dib Williams. In the fourth inning, Mickey Cochrane, Al Simmons, and Jimmie Foxx were successful in accomplishing this feat again.

Stolen bases have been an exciting part of baseball since its earliest days. However, in today's cautious and closely calculated Major League Baseball world, the art of stealing bases has now been elevated to a science and subject to scientific research. For example, Physicist David Kagan, California State University at Chico, conducted a series of scientific studies that helped him to determine that the three most important variables in base stealing are 1.) the runner's top speed; 2.) the jump—the lead isn't as important as many think; and 3.) the runner's speed when he reaches second base. To minimize the time when they begin to slow down, "base-runners slide past the base and grab it on their way by," Kagan says, noting that more and more players seem to be using this tactic.

As science takes over, the stolen base may be on its way to becoming an endangered species. Several managers believe that the risk-reward involved in this strategy is simply not worth the gamble. If this perception turns out to be true, it would likely mean that Rickey Henderson, with his 1,406 career steals (1979-2003) would forever seal his place in the record books as the greatest base stealer of all time.

CHAPTER FOUR
The Most Prized Play

"Defense is baseball's visible poetry and its invisible virtue."
—*Thomas Boswell, writer*

There's just something truly exciting about seeing an incredible play in baseball, especially if it is pulled off by your team. What's better than a home run? A walk-off home run. What's better than a walk-off home run? A walk-off grand slam. What could top a walk-off grand slam? An inside-the-park grand slam home run.

Do you know what's better than all of those? That would be the triple-play. But, what could possibly beat the triple-play for excitement? Well, believe it or not, there is one play and it is the most prized and rarest-of-the rare—the one that defies odds; the unassisted triple play by an outfielder. That's right, an outfielder recording all three outs in a single inning. Incredible!

The Triple Play

According to exceptional record keeping by the Society for American Baseball Research (SABR), there have been only 696 triple plays in Major League Baseball between 1876 and July 1, 2014. The triple play is relatively rare, since it requires at least two runners on base, no outs, and a batted ball hit in a way that allows the ball to be quickly and cleanly fielded so the batter, along with the two base runners, can be tagged out. The majority of triple plays take place in the infield with runners on first and second bases.

This author personally witnessed a triple play, while serving as the visiting team batboy for the New York Yankees, when they played the Washington Senators at Griffith Stadium. The date was May 22, 1953. In the top of the ninth, the Yankees had men on first and second with Irv Noren at the plate. The Yankees were trailing the Senators 12–4. Crouched just outside of the on-deck circle, I watched as Irv Noren ripped a blistering line drive straight to the pitcher, Bob Porterfield. Porterfield snared the ball and threw to first baseman Mickey Vernon to double-up the runner attempting to get back to first. Vernon then threw to Pete Runnels at second base for the third out. There it was—triple play! And I got to see this amazing feat up close!

Speaking of triple plays, here's an historic one. It was the first recorded 4-5-4[5] triple play ever executed in the Major Leagues. This record setting triple play took place in a game between the St. Louis Cardinals and the Pittsburg Pirates at the Pirates' PNC Park, on Saturday, May 9, 2015. With the Cardinals at-bat in the second inning, men on second and third, no outs, the batter, Yadier Molina, hit a rising line drive near second base. A split-second later, the base runner, Jason Heyward, took off sprinting full speed for third. Just as the ball was leaving the infield in what appeared to be a base hit, the second baseman, Neil Walker, made an outstanding catch (one out). He then fired the ball to third base to nail the runner, Jhonny Peralta, before Peralta could return to the bag (two outs). With two outs, several seconds of confusion occurred when the Pirates third baseman, Jung Ho Kang, thinking it was the third out, started walking off the infield towards the dugout. With those in the Pirates dugout yelling for Kang to throw the ball back to Walker before the base runner could safely return to second, Kang, still perplexed, finally got the message and threw the ball to Walker, who stepped on the base for the third and final out. The official scoring of this first-ever triple play pulled off between a second and third baseman was recorded as 4-5-4.

Remarkable Unassisted Triple Play

Even more unusual than a triple play that involves two players is an unassisted triple play; it's even rarer than a pitcher throwing a perfect game. This play is normally executed by an infielder, pitcher, or catcher. Only 15 players have completed this amazing feat. Neal Ball, playing shortstop for the Cleveland Naps, went into the record books on July 19, 1909, for being the first player in major league history to execute an unassisted triple play.

This amazing play took place in a game between the Naps and Boston Red Sox at Cleveland's League Park. According to *The Plain Dealer* newspaper, here's what happened: In the second inning, Amby McConnell hit a line drive directly over Naps pitcher, Cy Young's head; Neal Ball jumped up and speared the ball. He next stepped on second base to get Heinie Wagner, and then tagged Jake Stahl out, as he was running towards second base.

Photo: National Baseball Hall of Fame
Cleveland Naps shortstop Neal Ball (second from left) poses with (from left)
Amby McConnell, Heinie Wagner and Jack Stahl of Boston after Ball made
big-league baseball's first unassisted triple play on July 19, 1909.

It was reported that this first-ever play happened so quickly, the ballplayers on the field did not know the inning was over and the crowd of 11,000 were equally confused. In fact, Cy Young, the Naps starting pitcher, also confused, asked, "Where are you going, Neal?" Ball simply replied, "That's three outs." Once those fans in the ballpark realized what had happened, they gave Neal Ball a standing ovation, while his teammates applauded him as he returned to the dugout. In the next inning, Neal Ball hit an inside-the-park home run over Tris Speaker's head in deep center field (the only home run he would hit that season). The glove that Neal Ball used to make that unassisted triple play is on exhibit at the National Baseball Hall of Fame.

Including the above play on July 19, 1909, fourteen of these rarities have taken place during regular season games. As for the post season, Bill Wambsganss, second baseman for the Cleveland Indians, is largely remembered as the man who pulled off the only unassisted triple play in World Series history.

It was October 10, 1920, Game 5 of the World Series between the Cleveland Indians and the Brooklyn Robins. In the top of the fifth inning, Clarence Mitchell, the Robins' left-handed relief pitcher— also known for his strong batting skills—came to the plate to pinch-hit. Wambsganss intentionally moved back onto the outfield grass in order to keep any ball hit in his direction from getting through the infield and creating an opportunity for a run to score. Once the count reached one ball and one strike, the hit-and-run signal was given. Mitchell connected with a solid line drive that was moving several feet to the right of second base and headed towards center field. Wambsganss, seeing the runner (Kilduff) breaking for third, moved quickly towards the bag, just as the hit ball came in his direction. With his outstretched glove, Wambsganss caught the ball in mid-flight. The runner, Kilduff, was almost to third base and Miller, coming from first base was rapidly approaching second. Momentum carried Wambsganss in the direction he was headed and a couple of strides took him directly to second base. The moment he stepped on the bag, Kilduff was out. Miller's momentum carried him directly to Wambsganss. He was roughly five feet away, with no time to turn back. According to a January 22, 1966, article in *The Sporting News*, Wambsganss was quoted as saying, "He stopped running and stood there, so I just tagged him. That was all there was to it," Wambsganss explained. "Just before I tagged him, he said, 'Where'd you get that ball?' I said, Well, I've got it and you're out number three."

This unassisted triple play was executed in seconds. Three outs! Unsure of what they'd just witnessed, the crowd became silent, until they realized what had just taken place. Then the fans erupted in a torrent of appreciation. (In that same game, Elmer Smith, also of the Indians hit the first grand slam in World Series history.)

The fifteenth and most recent triple play (as of 2015) took place on Sunday, August 23, 2009, when Philadelphia Phillies' second-baseman Eric Bruntlett made an unassisted triple play against the New York Mets at Citi Field in New York to end the game.

This extremely rare play came in the ninth inning with the Mets trailing by two runs, but threatening with runners on first and second base and no outs. Both base runners were stealing on a 2-2 pitch when the Mets' batter, Jeff Francoeur, hit a line drive up the middle that appeared headed in the direction of center field for a single. Since the two runners were off and running on the 2-2 pitch, Bruntlett moved into position to cover second base; the ball was easily caught by Bruntlett and he quickly stepped on second base to double up Luis Castillo, and then tagged Daniel Murphy for out number three. This rare play went into the record books as the fifteenth unassisted triple play in major league history, and only the second triple play to actually end a ballgame.

The Most Prized Play

The rarest baseball play of all is the unassisted triple play by an outfielder. This unbelievable feat has been executed only once in professional baseball: On July 19, 1911, in a game between the Pacific Coast League's teams, the Vernon Tigers and the Los Angeles Angels. With the score tied at 3-3 in the sixth inning, and base runners on first and second, Walter Carlisle, center fielder for Vernon was forever enshrined in the record books when he made a spectacular diving catch of a short fly ball hit by Roy Akin.

With the batter and both runners receiving a "hit and run" sign from their coach, the two players on base took off at full speed on the pitch. Akin swung, hitting a short fly to just behind second base. Carlisle, also running as fast as possible, made a thrilling one-handed catch. His momentum caused him to tumble head-over-heels on the ground, and amazingly he returned to his feet in an upright position. With his balance regained, Carlisle raced to second base and immediately touched the sack for the second out to nail the lead runner, Charlie Moore, who by that time had rounded third and was headed to home plate. Now with two outs secured, Carlisle next shifted his direction and ran to first base where he stepped on the bag, making George Metzger— who was attempting to return to first base ahead of Carlisle—the third and final out. There you have it, a triple play by an outfielder; the rarest play in professional baseball.

Even though Walter Carlisle made an incredible catch that helped the Tigers to defeat the Los Angeles Angels by a score of 5 to 4, that catch was only incidental to this rarest of all plays.

The next day, *The Sporting News* reported that Carlisle had, at one point been a circus acrobat, which may have helped account for that extra athletic ability he showed in making the tumbling play. (On July 20, 1944, the *Pittsburg Post-Gazette* (Page 19) ran an article describing this play and reporting that a special ceremony was held at Wrigley Field, marking the thirty-third anniversary of Walter Carlisle's famous play and also honoring Harry A. Williams, one-time *Los Angeles Times'* sports editor whose description of the maneuver took five full columns of space the following day.)

CHAPTER FIVE

Not Just A Passing Fad

"I venture to say that not one of you cares a hoot about baseball but to me it is my very life." —*Grace Coolidge, First Lady of the United States (1923–1929)*

If you are a die-hard baseball fan, you may remember reading or hearing about the sporting-goods magnate, A.G. Spalding. If you are not one totally committed to knowing the history of baseball, Spalding created the controversial Mills Commission who studied the game, came up with what was perceived to be its origin as well as its alleged inventor, Abner Doubleday.

A.G. Spalding later proclaimed baseball to be not just an all-American sport, but also all-male: "A woman may take part in the grandstand, with applause for the brilliant play, with waving kerchief to the hero," he wrote in his 1911 book America's National Game, but she couldn't actually play: "Base Ball is too strenuous for womankind."

Spalding did little to make known a number of factual things about baseball, including how it actually came into being, whom truly invented it, and that women's involvement in the game could have easily been traced as far back as the 1830s.

Women played baseball in colleges, on amateur teams, and on barnstorming "Bloomer Girls" teams. By the fall of 1942, the all-male dominance of America's greatest pastime was being threatened by WWII; its sheer survival was at stake. How could baseball survive with so many professional ballplayers going off to war? One man came up with the solution, and women stepped up to the plate and pulled off the unimaginable.

Amazing Twelve-Year Ride

Ask practically anyone to name the approximate time that women first start playing organized baseball, and don't be surprised that their focus will be on the formation of the *All American Girls Professional Baseball League* shortly after the on-set of World War II, especially since that League's story made the big screen in *League of their Own*.

Well, WWII did play a major role in introducing women into the ranks of professional baseball—but only within the modern era. By the fall of 1942, young men, 18 years of age and over, being drafted into the armed services dealt a devastating blow to baseball, as player after player traded in their flannel uniforms for military khakis.

By 1943, some 340 major leaguers were in uniform, as well as more than 3,000 minor league players—so many, that several of the smaller leagues suspended operations for the duration of the war. With team rosters critically low, scouts searched everywhere for players to fill the void. Meanwhile, the major and minor league teams had to make do with whoever was available. With so many talented players absent from the diamond, the game was becoming little more than a ghost of the real sport.

In the fall of 1942, the War Department announced that Major League Baseball would probably have to suspend play through the spring and summer of 1943 due to the lack of available baseball players. After receiving that notification, team owners became concerned that Americans would have forgotten about baseball by the time the war ended. They knew professional baseball was in trouble, and that they faced a huge challenge:

How does one keep America's favorite pastime alive?

Philip K. Wrigley, chewing gum magnate and owner of the Chicago Cubs, came up with the answer—the *All-American Girls Professional Baseball League.*

Once operational, the *All-American Girls Professional Baseball League* (AAGPBL) existed for twelve seasons. It officially began play on May 30, 1943, and would cease operations at the end of the 1954 season. Historians blamed the end of the AAGPBL on a combination of factors, including shrinking local fan bases caused in part by the rise of other types of recreation and entertainment. By the early 1950's, Major League Baseball games were being televised. The unenthusiastic promotion of AAGPBL games and a decline in team owners' financial support and their inability to increase gate revenues also contributed. The game evolved into a purely hardball sport, and talented female baseball players were difficult to find.

The Early Years

Keep in mind that women actually started playing organized baseball much earlier than the formation of the AAGPBL—as far back as the 1800s. Information taken from the archives of the Library of Congress revealed that women's baseball teams existed as early as the mid-1860s at Vassar College in Poughkeepsie, New York. (The accompanying photograph is of Vassar College's 1876 baseball team named

"The Resolutes." Observe that those women players, while wearing baseball caps, were also wearing long dresses with long sleeves. Other important dates in the Library's data bank included: 1866: Formation of two women's baseball teams: the Laurel Base Ball Club and the Abenakis at Vassar Female College, Poughkeepsie, NY; 1867: First African-American women's team played in Philadelphia, PA; 1868: First non-collegiate women's team was organized in Peterborough, New Hampshire; and 1875, The first women's baseball game—for which fans were charged admission fees and women players were paid—took place between the "Blondes" and the "Brunettes" in Springfield, Illinois, on September 11.

By the end of the nineteenth century, women's baseball was growing in popularity as it became more of a competitive sport. Women player's uniforms also changed: Gone were those high-button shoes, high necklines, long skirts and long sleeves. They were replaced with Amelia Jenks Bloomer's loose fitting "bloomer" style trousers that carried her name. This new uniform attire brought with it a new breed of women baseball players known as the "Bloomer Girls." (Sometime later, most of the players would discard their bloomers in favor of standard baseball uniforms.)

These teams of "Bloomer Girls", although publicized as women's teams, were actually mixed; each team had at least one male player. (Allegedly, the great Hall of Famer, Rogers Hornsby, got his start on a Bloomer Girls team.)

There were no organized leagues. Teams from such cities as Boston and New York began 'barnstorming' from state to state, challenging local amateur, semi-pro, and minor league men's teams in front of thousands of spectators. For example, at a game in Boston in 1879, a crowd of 1,600 watched a women's team from New York play another women's team from Philadelphia.

The Bloomer Girls teams were not just a passing fad attempting to make their place in a traditionally all-male sport. Some of them played as early as the 1890s. They would continue on for about 40 years, and be synonymous with women's baseball.

During their era, the Bloomer Girls teams produced some outstanding stars, and talk of their existence actually encouraged other talented "tom-boyish baseball-loving" women to join local men's semi-pro teams. Many of these talented women had set their sights on playing professional baseball someday.

While most of the early players are unknown today, there were a handfull of women players who—*against all odds*—were able to at least put a crack—no matter how small—in the gender barrier of professional baseball.

The following are their stories:

Lizzie Arlington

One of the first highly talented women to step up to the plate was Elizabeth Stride or Stroud, who would later, become professionally known as Lizzie Arlington.

Claim to Fame: On July 5, 1898, Lizzie Arlington became the first woman to play professional (minor league) baseball.

Background:

Lizzie grew up in the coal-mining hills of Mahanoy City, Pennsylvania, where she played baseball with her father and brothers. Lizzie also gained inspiration from and was given pointers on pitching by John Elmer Stivetts, a pitching great who played eleven seasons of Major League Baseball.

According to an article in the July 3, 1898 edition of the *Philadelphia Inquirer,* Captain William J. Conner, well known in sporting and theatrical circles, heard of Lizzie, went out to see her play, and immediately offered her a salary of $100 per week to finish the season with his baseball team, the Philadelphia Reserves. In an effort to increase spectator attendance and gate receipts, Captain Conner had Stroud use the name Arlington, believing that a more English-sounding name would be better for promotional purposes.

Below are a few snippets taken from that article:

"Captain Conner is very proud of his new star and sees millions in her because of the novelty of a woman playing on a men's team. Unfortunately,

Arlington's pitching debut with the club at an exhibition game against Richmond on July 2, 1898, drew only 500 fans. Disappointed in the turnout, Captain Connor immediately released Lizzie from her contract. However, she was quickly signed to an Atlantic League contract by that league's president, and future Hall of Famer, Ed Barrow." Barrow, too, saw Arlington as a novelty draw, and Lizzie made her professional debut in a regular-season game on July 5, 1898—as a member of the Reading Coal Barons (aka Reading Coal Heavers). With her team winning 5-0 over the Allentown Peaches, Lizzie entered the game to pitch in the ninth inning. She gave up two hits and walked a batter to load the bases. Then she retired the next three batters to preserve the win.

With her brief appearance in that July 5th game, Lizzie Stride Stroud Arlington made baseball history as she became the first woman to ever play professional (minor league) baseball. (Her official appearance was documented in the box score from the game that was published in the July 16, 1898 issue of *The Sporting News*. That box score is on display at the National Baseball Hall of Fame.)

An article appearing in the *Reading Eagle* on the day following her debut made note that "Miss Arlington, along with several other persons, drove onto the grounds in a stylish carriage drawn by two white horses." Interestingly, the article also described Arlington as "a plump young woman with an attractive face and rosy cheeks. She wore a gray uniform with skirt coming to the knees, black stockings and a jaunty cap. Her hair was not cropped, but done up in the latest fashion."

While Lizzie Arlington was under contract with the Atlantic League, she was not assigned to any particular team; she was to be used as a "floater" to help teams promote that a woman would be playing, thereby increasing turn-out and gate revenues. This promotion strategy helps to explain the "A" (for Atlantic League) that is visible on Lizzie's blouse in the photograph taken by Gilbert & Bacon of Philadelphia, Pennsylvania.

To add creditability to the league's plan to move Lizzie from team to team, the *Hartford Courant* ran an article on July 6—the day after her single inning pitching appearance for the Reading Coal Heavers—reporting: "The Newarks will be here the balance of the week and a sensation is promised for Friday's game when Miss Lizzie Arlington will pitch for the Hartfords. It is said that she plays ball just like a man and talks ball like a man and if it was not for her bloomers she would be taken for a man on the diamond, having none of the peculiarities of women ballplayers."

Although Barrow took pleasure in the publicity that he received for having a woman baseball player on the field, the league's other teams did not share his passion. The Hartford Co-Operatives game was cancelled at the eleventh hour. The reason given was that the team was apprehensive that Lizzie Arlington's talents were not equal to those of the player she would be replacing. The Hartfords also believed that winning took priority over gate attendance. Other teams agreed and voiced their opposition. As a result, all other games planned for Lizzie in the Atlantic League did not materialize. While Ed Barrow allegedly said Lizzie Arlington did make appearances with Newark, Patterson, and Wilmington, no evidence was found that confirmed Barrow's statement.

Lizzie Arlington ended her brief minor league career after taking to the mound in the ninth inning of that July 5th game for Reading (PA) of the Atlantic League and dropped out of the news after failing to draw the anticipated crowds to those games publicizing her appearance.

Those failures did not mean the end of Lizzie's baseball career. She continued to headline barnstorming tours with the Bloomer Girls as "Miss Lizzie Arlington, The Famous Lady Pitcher"—for a number of years afterwards.

In spite of the hullabaloo—brief as it was—Lizzie Arlington played in only one inning of minor league baseball. Yet, her sole appearance on July 5, 1898, made it official; Lizzie Arlington carved her notch in baseball's record books for becoming the first woman to play professional (minor league) baseball.

Lizzie Arlington died in 1919, as a result of complications following surgery.

Lizzie "Spike" Murphy

While Lizzie Arlington is recognized as the first woman to play baseball professionally, albeit in the minor leagues, it would take another twenty-four years before public recognition would be bestowed upon Lizzie "Spike" Murphy.

Claim to Fame: On August 14, 1922, Lizzie Murphy became the first woman to professionally play hardball against a Major League Baseball team.

One thing that I have learned as a writer is that baseball legends can often be clouded by inaccuracies that tend to grow and become more acceptable with each telling. This was the difficulty that I encountered when researching Lizzie Murphy. Various resources differed in their descriptions of those events surrounding Lizzie's background, as well as her history-making accomplishments. In order to provide the most accurate information possible about Lizzie Murphy, I decided to rely primarily on input from three reputable resources: The Rhode Island Heritage Hall of Fame (founded in March 1965), which inducted Lizzie Murphy into their Hall in 1994; the Exploratorium Museum, San Francisco, California; and a 1965 Sports Illustrated article by author John Hanlon. I send my appreciation to each.

Background:

As the story goes, Lizzie Murphy could best be described as a tomboy who loved baseball. Early in her life, Lizzie dropped her Christian name, Elizabeth, and preferred that she be called just plain "Lizzie" or "Spike." Lizzie Murphy was as at home on the baseball field—at first base —as any male player. In the field, Lizzie wore her reddish-blonde hair tightly wound around her head and tucked under her peaked cap. Yes, Lizzie Murphy was a tomboy in every sense of the word. At 5 feet 6 inches tall, her playing weight was a solid 120 pounds, and she could keep up with most men when it came to fielding, throwing, and running. Perhaps, Lizzie's only flaw was an understandable lack of power when she swung the bat. When in the field and playing defense, "Spike" chattered constantly in the fashion of ballplayers who possessed that "ole p*ss and vinegar"—yes, Lizzie Murphy was there to play the game!

On those days when Lizzie would show up to play in men's "choose-up" games, she was the first choice of team captains. By age fifteen, Lizzie was playing with such prestigious amateur teams as the Warren Silk Hats and the Warren Baseball Club; she was a rising star.

Lizzie also learned quickly that it paid to have good business sense when it came to earning money. You might say that she—at age eighteen—became the first female holdout in baseball history. In her first appearance as a paid professional for a Warren Rhode Island semipro team, Lizzie learned that it was customary pass a hat among those attending the game. She became aware that a fairly nice sum of $85 had been collected for the players to share amongst themselves. However, when the pot was divvyed up between players, Lizzie was somehow overlooked; she received not a single penny. Convinced that her presence and play had helped her team enhance the amount of money collected, Lizzie Knew she had been taken advantage of. She chose not to complain or make a scene, but she had learned a good lesson. Never again would she allow something like this to happen a second time.

Lizzie had a plan! She knew the team was scheduled to play in Newport the following Saturday. With her as an attraction in this navy base town, lots of sailors would likely be attending the game. She had overheard her team's manager bragging that he was looking forward to a collection that would likely produce one of his better jackpots.

Lizzie did as expected. All week long she practiced with the team and said not a single word about finances. Saturday morning, as the team was getting ready for the trip to Newport, she simply said four *powerful* words to the manager, "No money, no Newport." The manager, surprised, but without hesitation, quickly agreed to pay her $5 per game, plus an equal share of the collection. With that encounter, Lizzie knew that she was maturing in ways of playing the game, both on and off the field.

As talk of Lizzie's talents became widespread, so did her marketability. With an offer of additional money, she joined the Providence Independents around 1918, and began touring southern New England. Some years later, the All-Stars of Boston signed Lizzie to a contract. As part of the agreement, she not only received even greater pay, she was allowed to go into the stands and sell autographed picture postcards of herself in uniform.

Lizzie "Spike" Murphy, also known as the "Queen of Baseball," reached the pinnacle of her career on August 14, 1922, when the Boston All-Stars team, of which she was a member, played an exhibition against the Boston Red Sox. Lizzie entered the game to the crowd's cheers and boos, and performed well at first base. As a result of that appearance, Lizzie Murphy took her place in baseball history, officially becoming the first woman to play against a major league team. Unfortunately, Lizzie Murphy never got to bat in that game.

According to various legends, Lizzie would go on to have two more re-cord-setting "firsts." In 1928, she played on a National League all-star team in a game against the Boston Braves, and became the first person of either gender to play for all-star teams in both the American and National leagues. Next, according to unverified legend, Lizzie purportedly became the first woman to play in the Negro Leagues. Multiple (questionable) stories allege that she played first base for a team known as the Cleveland Colored Giants when they came through Rhode Island. Unfortunately, from what this writer could determine around that time, there were at least four teams that used the name Cleveland Giants or Colored Giants. (No evidence was found substan-tiating that Lizzie Murphy was a member of any Negro League team.)

It was further reported—never confirmed—that Lizzie got a hit off of the legendary Negro League pitcher and future National Baseball Hall of Famer, Satchel Paige. As part of this unverified story goes, when the great Negro League star Josh Gibson, was asked if Paige had gone easy on Lizzie, Gibson allegedly replied, "Satch didn't want to be charged with a hit by a woman of any color."

In 1935, and at the age of forty, Lizzie Murphy retired from baseball. Two years later she married, but her husband met with an untimely death a few years afterwards. With little money left from her baseball days, Lizzie worked at various jobs, including in mills and on oyster boats, to help support her mother and herself.

Lizzie "Spike" Murphy died on April 17, 1964, at the age of 70.

Marcenia "Toni" Stone

There it was— bright as day—a November 10, 1996 article in the sports section of *The New York Times* newspaper leading with an attention-grabbing headlines, **"Toni Stone, 75, First Woman To Play Big-League Baseball."** Naturally, that bold title got this writer's attention. I had always read and heard that the legendary Lizzie "Spike" Murphy was the first female to participate in a major league ballgame, and that she was also the first woman to play in the Negro Leagues. The first paragraph of this article by Robert McG. Thomas Jr. cast serious doubt on what I previously was led to believe. The words were captivating: "Toni Stone, a scrappy second baseman who became a footnote to baseball history in 1953 as a member of the Negro League's Indianapolis Clowns when she became the first woman to play as a regular on a big-league professional team, died on Nov. 2 at a nursing home in Alameda, Calif. She was 75 and had lived in Oakland, Calif., for many years."

Another part of the article added, "She may have been hired as a novelty, but Stone's historic career was enough to earn her induction into the Women's Sports Foundation's International Women's Sports Hall of Fame in 1985. Allegedly, she had her moments, none more memorable than the exhibition game in Omaha on Easter Sunday in 1953, when it was said that the opposing pitcher strolled through the Clowns' locker room mockingly asking the players how they would like him to pitch to them, slow, medium or fast. 'Any way you like,' Stone told him after she had dressed in the umpire's locker room. 'Just don't hit me.'

It was, as she never tired of recalling, a fastball he delivered that she hit over the pitcher's head into center field. She was so excited she could barely make it to first base. No wonder. The pitcher was Satchel Paige and her's was the only hit off him that day.

[Toni Stone], the woman who broke the sex barrier in baseball played in men's amateur leagues until she was 60. Satchel Paige would have approved."

Now as a non-fiction writer, if there's one thing that I've learned from doing in-depth research, it that it is fairly common to find conflicting stories and misinformation about ball players, especially those playing decades earlier in both the Major Leagues and Negro Leagues.

Many times, even the events as to what actually happened are contradictory and/or unclear. With that said, there appears to be enough evidence (unlike Lizzie Murphy's proof) for me to believe that Toni Stone did become the first woman to play in the Negro American League when she took the field in 1953. However, I must challenge the accuracy of that portion of the story saying that Stone got a hit off Satchel Paige during an exhibition game in Omaha on Easter Sunday 1953. If you remember—as I have said elsewhere in this book—in 1953, I was visiting team batboy for the Washington Senators. In that position, I served as batboy for the St. Louis Browns, and Satchel Paige was a member of that team. The Browns did not play the Indianapolis Clowns in Omaha or anywhere else. As noted in my book, Baseball's Finest Moments, I had developed a nice friendship with Satchel Paige, and can verify the fact that he was playing for the St. Louis Browns. As confirmation to the accuracy of my statement, an article that appears on the SABR website about Toni Stone, clearly notes that "a check of the St. Louis newspapers in March and April of 1953, shows that the Browns did not play any exhibition games against the Clowns in spring training that year. It is possible that Stone faced Paige at another time, although it is not clear whether such a matchup ever occurred."

Toni Stone became one of the first women to play as a regular on a big-league professional team when she joined the Negro Leagues' Indianapolis Clowns in 1953. It is said that her predecessor at second base for the Clowns was Hank Aaron, who signed with the Milwaukee Braves after the 1952 season.

In 1985 Stone was inducted into the Women's Sports Foundation's International Women's Sports Hall of Fame, and in 1990 she was included in two exhibits at the National Baseball Hall of Fame; one on "Women in Baseball" and another on "Negro League Baseball."

In 1990, Stone's hometown of Saint Paul, Minnesota, declared March 6 "Toni Stone Day." In 1993, she was inducted into the Women's Sports Hall of Fame, as well as the Sudafed International Women's Sports Hall of Fame. In her honor, Saint Paul, Minnesota named a ball field after her; it is located at the Dunning Baseball Complex.

Toni Stone died in 1996 in Oakland, California.

Now that you have read those similarities and claims regarding Lizzie Murphy's experiences and accomplishments in the Negro Leagues in comparison to those of Toni Stone —I want to remind you that likely much of these two stories' rhetoric was in part by design, as each baseball organization wanted to enhance the marketability of their female star player in order to increase gate attendance and revenues.

It's up to you to determine which portions of each of those stories you choose to believe.

CHAPTER SIX

Did She, Didn't She?

"To a pitcher, a base hit is the perfect example of negative feedback."
—Steve Hovley

Take a look at the above 1931 Library of Congress photo.

This author discovered the above photo while researching Babe Ruth. Sure, most every true baseball fan will quickly recognize these Yankee greats, Babe Ruth and Lou Gehrig. But, who are the other two? The young lady clothed in a professional looking baseball uniform, shaking hands with "The Babe", and the older man who could easily pass for a baseball dignitary, or a public figure. There must be some story here? Let's check it out!

This chapter contains one of the game's most mystifying events that even today continue to intrigue die-hard baseball fans. No, this "believe-it-or not" story didn't impact the outcome of a game, nor was it special enough to be captured in the official record books of Major League Baseball. However, what took place in a barnstorming pre-season game between the New York Yankees and their AA minor league baseball club, the Chattanooga Lookouts, on April 2, 1931, earned its place in baseball history as one of the most fascinating and legendary tales of all time.

Did She or Didn't She?

Perhaps it is best to start by introducing the young lady in the photo. Her name is Virne Beatrice "Jackie" Mitchell.

Early Years

Jackie Mitchell's birthday was August 29. Sources vary as to whether the year of her birth was 1912, 1913, or 1914. The daughter of Virne Wall Mitchell and Dr. Joseph Mitchell of Memphis, Tennessee, Jackie weighed three-and-one-half pounds at birth. When Jackie was old enough to walk her dad began to teach her the fundamentals of baseball, by teaching her how to catch and throw a ball. As Jackie grew and her physical abilities matured, she developed into an all-around athlete who excelled in a variety of sports including, basketball, boxing, and tennis. Baseball was her favorite.

It was as if fortune smiled on Jackie. In addition to her natural athletic abilities and dad's teaching, the "icing-on-the-cake" turned out to be Jackie's next door neighbor, future Baseball Hall of Famer, Dazzy Vance, the major league's premier strikeout pitcher during the 1920s. Vance was most impressed with Jackie's love for the game and her dedication to becoming proficient at playing baseball. He taught her a variety of pitching fundamentals including the windup and side-arm delivery; control in placing the ball on target; ways to identify a batter's weaknesses; and how to throw what would become her trademark "drop ball" (a pitch known today as a sinker). One report alleged that Jackie was only five or six years old when she learned how to throw that pitch. Vance also predicted that Jackie Mitchell would become a great ballplayer; one who could easily compete with men in men's leagues.

The P.T. Barnum of Baseball

The Mitchell family moved to Chattanooga where Jackie played in sandlot games as a teenager. When she turned sixteen, she played for an all-women's team. At seventeen, she attended a baseball camp in Georgia. It was March 1931. It was here that Joe Engle, the older man in the photo and the owner of the Chattanooga Lookouts first noticed Jackie. He was impressed. So much so, that Engle immediately signed the lefthander to a contract to play for the Lookouts; the class AA minor league team of the New York Yankees.

Joe Engle was much more than a baseball team's owner. He was known by many as the "P.T. Barnum of baseball" because of his showmanship and promotional skills...anything to draw more paying fans into his stadium. Once on Opening Day, Engle had his players enter the field riding on elephants; another time, he traded a shortstop for a turkey, roasted it, and served it to local sportswriters who had been "giving him the bird." Engel also raffled off cars and houses. His promotions were a big hit and fans turned out in droves to watch those games.

Once Jackie Mitchell was signed on March 28, 1931, Engel figured that he had come up with a winning combination that would bring crowds of spectators into Engel Stadium. During the off-season, he had booked the New York Yankees to play two exhibition games against the Lookouts. The games were to be played in April, as the Yankees barnstormed their way north from spring training in Florida. Getting Jackie Mitchell under contract left little, if any, doubt as to why; she was signed to attract publicity and generate ticket sales, both of which Engle would achieve.

Just prior to the game, Jackie posed for this photo with Ruth and Gehrig.

67

The scene was now set for another of Joe Engel's greatest promotions. Fans could not only witness the Yankees' famous "Murderers Row" in action, they were told that the Lookouts was the only minor league team in history to have a female on the mound. This claim was inaccurate – Lizzie Arlington had broken through in 1898.

The first game of this exhibition was scheduled to start on April Fool's Day, Wednesday, April 1st. Could scheduling Jackie Mitchell to pitch on that particular day have been another of Joe Engle's gimmicks?

We'll never know as that game was cancelled because of rain; play would resume the following day.

On Thursday, April 2, 1931—just five days after her signing—Jackie Mitchell made her first professional baseball appearance, with a crowd of 4,000 paid fans and scores of newspaper reporters and photographers pouring through the turnstiles to see if Mitchell could hold her own against the mighty "Bronx Bombers" Murderers Row. To the disappointment of many, Jackie Mitchell would not be the Lookouts starting pitcher; that assignment went to Clyde Barfoot.

Once the game was underway, Barfoot quickly gave up a double off the center field wall to the Yankees lead-off batter, Earle Combs. Next up, Lyn Lary stepped to the plate. Although he didn't wield a powerful bat, Lary slapped a sharp single up the middle that scored Combs from second base. With Chattanooga already behind by a run after facing only two batters, the Lookouts manager, Bert Niehoff, wasted no time in signaling for relief pitcher, Jackie Mitchell to come into the game.

Mitchell clad in a custom-made baggy white uniform, made her way to the mound to face the first batter of her baseball career—the "Sultan of Swat," Babe Ruth. A quick glance over at the on-deck circle, told Mitchell her next batter following Ruth would be the great Lou Gehrig.

"Babe Ruth stepped into the batter's box, and tipped his hat to the girl on the mound, and assumed an easy batting stance," a reporter wrote. "Mitchell went into her motion, winding her left arm 'as if she were turning a coffee grinder.' Then, with a side-armed delivery, she threw her signature pitch, "the drop." Ruth let it pass for a ball. At Mitchell's second delivery, Ruth 'swung and missed the ball by a foot.' He also missed the next one, and asked the umpire to inspect the ball. Then, with the count 1-2, Ruth watched as Mitchell's pitch caught the outside corner for a called strike three. Flinging his bat down in disgust, Babe Ruth retreated to the dugout." Next up to the plate was Lou Gehrig, who would finish the 1931 season with a batting average of .341, and also tie Babe Ruth for the league's lead in home runs. Gehrig swung at and missed three straight pitches. Mitchell walked the next batter, Tony Lazzeri. With that, the Lookouts manager pulled Jackie from the game." The New York Yankees went on to trounce the Lookouts, 14-4.

After throwing a total of seven pitches Jackie Mitchell had fanned the "Sultan of Swat" AND the "Iron Horse," back-to-back. In that exhibition game, Jackie Mitchell had pitched her way into the annals of baseball, and secured a place for her photograph to become a fixture in the National Baseball Hall of Fame.

Controversy

Within days after that game, a widely circulated and unverified rumor surfaced saying that Baseball Commissioner, Kenesaw Mountain Landis, had voided Mitchell's contract on the grounds that baseball was too strenuous for women. (Allegedly, a single reporter was believed to be the source of this unverified rumor.)

The story of Jackie Mitchell's nearly unbelievable accomplishment created a number of controversies, including a few that carried forth into the twenty-first century. First, newspapers were merciless: While there was much publicity surrounding this event, very little was positive towards this female ballplayer. Here are a few snippets allegedly published: The *New York Daily News:* "The Yankees will meet a club here that has a girl pitcher named Jackie Mitchell, who has a swell change of pace and swings a mean lipstick. I suppose that in the next town the Yankees enter they will find a squad that has a female impersonator in left field, a sword swallower at short, and a trained seal behind the plate. Times in the South are not only tough but silly." The *Baltimore Sun:* "As Ruth strutted to the plate, Chattanooga's manager called for the "snip-nosed blue-eyed girl." The *Baltimore Sun's* reporter apparently couldn't resist taking more cheap shots at Jackie for being a female. Included within the article, "Lou [Gehrig] could hear Jackie's girlfriends squealing delightedly." Not to be outdone, the *Washington Post* put more than their two cents into this ganging upon fray: "Without so much as powdering her nose or seeing if her lipstick was on straight, Jackie strode to the mound." Another demeaning shot was fired by that same *Washington Post* reporter: "Jackie probably remembered by that time that she was a woman and after all the excitement she undoubtedly wanted to go off and have a good cry so they let her retire from the game."

Over the decades a variety of comments from others, including well known baseball authorities have continued to flourish, including comments that the two strikeouts were staged. If Ruth and Gehrig were in on an orchestrated stunt, they never admitted it. Mitchell—for her part—held to her belief that she'd genuinely struck out the two Yankees. "Why, hell, they were trying, damn right," she said of Ruth and Gehrig not long before her death in 1987.

John Thorn, the official historian for Major League Baseball said that he believes "Ruth and Gehrig were in cahoots with the Lookouts' president and went along with the strikeout stunt, which did no harm to their reputations. The whole thing was a jape, a jest, a Barnumesque prank," he said. "Jackie Mitchell striking out Ruth and Gehrig is a good story for children's books, but it belongs in the pantheon with the Easter Bunny and Abner Doubleday 'inventing' baseball."

Fighting Controversy

Mitchell's unusual baseball career in a men's world wasn't over. In an era before televised games, when African-Americans as well as women, were unofficially barred from Major League Baseball, Jackie Mitchell found her pursuit of the sport she loved...difficult, at best. She started playing with various amateur teams after her magnificent outing against the mighty Yankees.

According to a June 27, 1931 article in the *Atlanta Constitution*, Jackie Mitchell's father said that she'd already traveled 3,000 miles and pitched in thirty-two games that summer.

In 1933, Jackie joined the highly popular men's baseball team called House of David (HOD). This team played up to 180 games per year and traveled extensively throughout the U.S. and into Canada. Chaperoned by her mother, Jackie traveled with the HOD team, and (allegedly) in one game she pitched against the National League's St. Louis Cardinals. According to a news report, the "nomadic House of David ball team, beards, girl pitcher and all, came, saw, and conquered the Cardinals, 8 to 6." *(Note: This writer was unable to identify creditable evidence that Jackie Mitchell did pitch for the House of David in a game against the St. Louis Cardinals. I did find references indicating that the great female athletic, Babe Didrikson, pitched on a few occasions against major league teams, but mostly in exhibition games for the House of David.)*

In 1937, Jackie Mitchell retired from baseball after purportedly indicating that she was sick of the circus-like atmosphere she encountered. At the age of twenty-four, she went to work for her father's optical business in Tennessee. Furthermore, Jackie refused to come out of retirement when the All-American Girls Professional Baseball League was formed in 1943, and they wanted to sign her as a player. However, Jackie did throw out the ceremonial first pitch for her old team, the Chattanooga Lookouts in 1982.

Jackie Mitchell died in Georgia on January 7, 1987.

Did Jackie Mitchell legitimately strike out both Babe Ruth and Lou Gehrig, or did the "P.T. Barnum of baseball" stage it as part of a ruse? What do you think? It's your call!

CHAPTER SEVEN

Incomprehensible Plate Appearances

"It's a round ball and a round bat and you got to hit it square."
—Joe Schultz

Decades ago, baseball clowns were legitimate players that entertained fans with their comedy and trick routines before and during games.

When Baseball Was Really Fun—*A Lost Tradition*

Major League Baseball games are not as entertaining as they were in decades past. Sure, there are those team mascots such as the San Diego Chicken; Philadelphia Phillies' Philly Phanatic; Arizona Diamondbacks' Baxter the Bobcat; Oakland A's Stomper and approximately thirty others. While their jobs differ, you are likely to see someone dressed in a weird and oversized costume running around delighting crowds by performing such stunts as dancing on dugouts, hugging anyone in sight, clumsily sliding on skateboard ramps, or dancing when a home team player hits a home run.

Back Then

Long before the New York Mets' mascot Mr. Met came on the scene in 1964, a few baseball players with diversified talents, created loads of fun at the ball park by performing a variety of antics and showing off their skills at home plate, in the field, and along the foul lines. That was entertainment!

These side attractions brought robust increases in gate revenues. After two seasons of being involved with both baseball and football games at Griffith Stadium, I was well aware of the power that special events, giveaways and clowns' activities could have on drawing and entertaining crowds; these promotions worked. I also knew that, without exception, those team owners whom I had the privilege of meeting, wanted their fans to laugh and have a good time at the ballpark—even if the hometown gang didn't emerge victorious.

Back then baseball clown headliners included:

The "father" of baseball clowns, *Germany Schaefer.* Schaefer debuted as a player in the big leagues on October 5, 1901, after signing with the Chicago Cubs. Bouncing from one team to another, he finally ended up playing infield for the Detroit Tigers in 1905. Germany Schaefer always enjoyed performing in front of crowds, and on June 24, 1906, he successfully pulled off his most historic act. Schaefer was called on to pinch hit with two outs in the bottom of the ninth, one runner on base, and his Tigers down by a run. He stepped up to the plate, Germany announced to the crowd[6]: "Ladies and gentlemen, you are now looking at Herman Schaefer, better known as 'Herman the Great,' acknowledged by one and all to be the greatest pinch-hitter in the world. I am now going to hit the ball into the left field bleachers. Thank you."

Facing Chicago's Doc White, Schaefer proceeded to hit the first pitch into the left field bleachers for a game-winning homer. Making his way around the diamond, Germany allegedly slid into every base, announcing his progress as if it were a horse race as he went around. "Turning into the back stretch, it's Schaefer by a length!" After hook-sliding into home, he popped up, doffed his cap, bowed, and said, "Ladies and Gentlemen, this concludes this afternoon's performance. I thank you for your kind attention."

As you remember in reading Chapter Three, Germany Schaefer also was the pioneer in the art of stealing first base.

When Schaefer died on May 16, 1919, at the age of forty-two, Detroit sportswriter Malcolm W. Bingay eulogized: "Germany Schaefer was the soul of baseball itself with all its sorrows and joys, the born troubadour of the game."

Jackie Price, played his way through the minor leagues as a shortstop, and at age thirty-three, he broke into Major League Baseball on August 18, 1946. His playing career with the Cleveland Indians was short. He appeared in only seven games, produced three hits, and played his final game on September 20, 1946.

Cleveland's management liked Price. Rather than cut him totally from the organization, they reassigned him as a "coach" in the minor leagues. After languishing close to a decade in the minors, Price recognized that his baseball career was coming to an end. He loved baseball and desperately wanted to maintain some role in the game. Searching for a solution, teammates remind-ed Price how he often entertained them with a variety of body maneuvers and uncanny contortions on the field and at-bat. At last, Price had discovered his ticket to staying in professional baseball—use those remarkable skills to amuse fans, in contrast to other performers who relied on comic routines to draw laughs.

One of Price's most famous tricks was to hang upside down and take batting practice. Batting either right-handed or left-handed, Price, suspended from the backstop or a pole by his ankles, would hit fastball pitches. Another stunt involved him shooting a baseball out of an air gun, then jumping into a jeep, and speeding into the outfield to catch the dropping ball. His arsenal included batting two balls with a fungo bat (light bat used in practice only) at the same time, sending them in opposite directions. Price's catching abilities were equally amazing[7]. He could catch baseballs between his legs, behind his back, and even in the neck of his uniform jersey. In Price's repertoire was a maneuver where he would place three baseballs in his throwing hand and toss them in a single motion to three different players stationed around the infield. During the 1940s and 1950s, Jackie Price entertained baseball fans throughout the major and minor leagues, charging $500 per game in MLB, and lesser fees in the minors. Jackie Price and another top-notch showman, Max Patkin, briefly teamed up as "clown coaches" for Bill Veeck's 1947 Cleveland Indians. Together, they proved to be a big crowd draw. Boston Red Sox manager Lou Boudreau described them as the "funniest show I ever saw."

According to *Baseball-Reference.Com*, Jackie Price resided in San Francisco, CA for the final seven years of his life. He maintained his flamboyant image (Price was renowned for his colorful dress shirts, and ties) and worked as a bartender. Having suffered from depression for the last years of his life, Price was found hanging from a light fixture with a leather belt around his neck when he was fifty-four. An autopsy revealed that he was intoxicated. His blood-alcohol level was .028 at time of death. The medical report indicated that Jackie Price committed suicide on October 2, 1967.

Nick Altrock was another of the "clowning kings." Back in the early 1950s, I had the privilege of spending some fun time with Nick Altrock, a longtime coach (1912-1953) with the Washington Senators. I always enjoyed listening to him tell stories of the past, and on occasion Nick would entertain me by performing a couple of his attention-getting baseball juggling acts. A couple of the older players with the Senators told stories about Nick's playing days that surprised me. I had given no thought to Nick's baseball talents. I was amazed to learn that in the early 1900s, Nick Altrock was one of baseball's finest left-handed pitchers. I also learned that in 1924, when Nick was a part-time player/coach for the Washington Senators, and as a batter, he became the oldest player at forty-eight to ever hit a triple. In 1933, at age fifty-seven, he became oldest player to ever appear in a game, making an unsuccessful attempt to pinch-hit. I gained a better perspective on Nick's lengthy baseball career as a player/coach when I learned that until the 1930s, the Senators generally let Nick play in one of the games at the end of the year. Thus his accomplishments in 1924 and 1933.

Now here's another (unconfirmed) story that defies reality, even if true: In 1901, Nick, pitching for Los Angeles in the California League, faced seven batters in a row. Being the showman he was, he intentionally walked all seven. According to legend, he then picked off six of those seven runners when they took their lead off first base.

My boss, Isadore Siegel, (visiting team's clubhouse manager, who also lived near Altrock when he "wintered" in Sarasota, FL) told me that Altrock's professional career as a pitcher was over around 1909, but it was his "second career" that made him famous. Nick Altrock became one of the most popular and longest working baseball clowns of all time.

Siegel said he had heard that Altrock, as a comic coach, drew a salary that rivaled Babe Ruth's. Nick continued as a coach and clown for the Washington Senators until 1953, when he turned seventy-six. Nick Altrock died on January 20, 1965 in Washington, D.C. at the age of eighty-eight.

Setting those old clowning routines aside, you may wonder: *Where has all the fun and excitement gone?* It's there, but today you have to find it. First of all, don't expect to be enamored by seeing a MLB player taking to the diamond to do anything that remotely resembles those fun acts performed by past clown players. It isn't going to happen! However, if you are in the right ballpark, you may be entertained by the likes of mascots such as the Phillie Phanatic or San Diego Chicken—all for fun, and sometimes to raise money for a charity.

Baseball being baseball, there's no escaping what a creative promoter might do to get more people into the stands. Today's MLB ballparks offer plenty: team museums, apparel and knickknacks shops, concession stands with choices from traditional hotdogs, beer, peanuts, and Cracker Jacks to vegetarian-friendly foods (and everything in between). But, baseball's allure is the potential for something captivating happening in the game that will never be duplicated.

Here are a few of the most bizarre things that have taken place inside the batter's box:

One-Eighth

In 1951, Bill Veeck, the new owner of the St. Louis Browns, an American League team, was well aware of his primary challenge—get more people into his ballpark. Attendance was extremely poor. Even the visiting teams complained that their share of the gate receipts did not even cover travel expenses.

Veeck, while owner of a triple-A minor league team and the major league's Cleveland Indians, had built a reputation as a visionary and a solid promoter. He loved to make baseball fun, even when his team was losing. On his first night as owner of the Browns, Veeck surprised everyone in attendance with a free beer or soda, but knew it would take much more than a free drink to get people into the stands to watch his second-rate ball club. He needed to come up with something different—something dramatic. In this moment of desperation, Veeck looked at his possibilities. He knew 1951 was the fiftieth anniversary of the American League. His radio sponsor, Falstaff Brewery, had distributors and dealers throughout the state. Perhaps he could hype the League's anniversary and tie it in with something from Falstaff to increase the number of people coming through the turnstiles. Veeck, creative juices flowing, came up with an idea that would send shock waves throughout the baseball world, and fans would absolutely love it. A birthday party! That's right, a birthday celebration for both the American League and Falstaff Brewery. Such a connection would bring Falstaff increased publicity, and the

Browns would benefit by having Falstaff's staff and distributors hustling tickets all over the state. Next question, what was Falstaff's real anniversary date? No one at Falstaff knew the answer, and Veeck was pleased with this feedback. He confidentially remarked, "If we couldn't prove it fell on the day we chose, neither could anyone prove it didn't. The day we chose gave us a Sunday doubleheader against the last-place Detroit Tigers." Veeck promised Falstaff's top executives that he would do something so original and spectacular the brewery would receive national publicity. When pressed for details, he refused to divulge his secret but did say his idea was so explosive that he could not afford to take the slightest chance of a leak. Veeck later admitted in his book, *Veeck as in Wreck*, that he did not have a plan. "What can I do, I asked myself, that is so spectacular that no one will be able to say he had seen it before?"

On Sunday, August 19, 1951, Bill Veeck, in his fun-loving way, pulled his most famous stunt. He sent Eddie Gaedel, three feet, seven inches tall and weighing only sixty-five pounds, to bat as a pinch hitter in the first inning of the second game of the double-header being played in St. Louis.

As Veeck had anticipated, the umpire immediately challenged the legality of sending Gaedel into the game. The Browns were prepared: Manager Zack Taylor readily produced Gaedel's signed contract. Veeck had also mailed a copy to the American League office, but late enough to ensure that it would not be received prior to game time. The head umpire was left with little choice but to allow the substitution. Once cleared to play, the tiny man squeezed into a deep crouch at home plate, displaying a strike zone slightly larger than a matchbox. The crowd loved it, and players from both teams had fun. Veeck later said his greatest concern in pulling off this stunt was that Gaedel would swing at the ball and unluckily hit an easy out. He said he threatened to "shoot" Gaedel if he swung the bat.

Since I had a recollection of this weird situation—as told to me by one of baseball's greatest pitchers ever—Satchel Page, I thought you might enjoy Satchel's version of what took place. He should know. In between the double-header games, several different entertainment activities were going on, including one that featured Satchel on the drums performing at home plate. Satchel stopped the show, cold!

Here is how I remember Satchel Paige's version of Eddie Gaedel's most memorable day—one that shall forever live in baseball history.

In his typically hilarious way, Satchel, eyes dancing, hands waving, created the scene by capturing the party atmosphere in the St. Louis Browns stands and on the field the moment Eddie Gaedel jumped out of one of those big, fake birthday cakes. Gaedel, dressed in his little St. Louis Browns' uniform, immediately ran from the "cake" into the dugout. Fans knew something was up; they just didn't know what. In the second game of the double-header the Browns came to bat in the bottom half of the first inning and the announcer proclaimed a pinch hitter for the leadoff batter, Frank Saucier. At that point, tiny Eddie Gaedel came marching out of the dugout, bat in hand, and went directly to the plate. On the back of his uniform shirt was the number "1/8"—big and bold—for all in the stands to see.

Satchel, in his animated way, created a picture of the hysterical scene—players doubling over with laughter, fans screaming and applauding, the home plate umpire revealing shock and disbelief, and then charging toward the Browns' dugout questioning the legitimacy of this substitution. Satchel gestured wildly, suggesting the uproar among the 18,000 fans, and described the scene of Detroit's catcher, Bob Swift, dropping down onto his knees in an effort to create a miniscule target for the pitcher, Bob Cain. At this point, Satchel said, the place was a madhouse. After trying to throw two pitches to the little man, Cain was laughing so hard he could barely throw the ball to the plate. As only Satchel could do, he demonstrated the pitcher's windups and deliveries. After four balls were thrown—one way or the other—Gaedel walked to first. He was immediately relieved by a pinch runner, but Satchel said the fun continued, giving a demonstration of how Gaedel clowned his way back to the Browns' dugout.

Afterwards, William Harridge, president of the American League intervened, and Gaedel was forced to retire with an on-base percentage of 1.000. Major League Baseball's official rules were also changed, noting that all player contracts must be approved in advance of that player actually appearing in a game.

No one had ever seen the likes of Gaedel at the plate, and it is unlikely that anyone ever will. It turned out Eddie Gaedel was an actor. He had been hired, of course, by the Browns' creative owner, Bill Veeck, who loved to bring fun and excitement to baseball.

Eddie Gaedel's uniform shirt with the number "1/8" is on display in the National Baseball Hall of Fame.

It is doubtful that anyone will ever top Eddie's plate appearance, or overthrow his record for the weirdest at-bat ever to take place in an official Major League Baseball game, but some keep trying.

Batter Up!

Major league players have stepped up to the plate during official games literally thousands upon thousands of times since the game's inception. For example, the years 2009 - 2012 each had over 165,000 at-bats per season. With such numbers a fan will witness some of the best to worst circumstances, as batter after batter, attempts to reach first base safely.

The Oddest

Santiago Casilla originally signed with the Oakland A's on January 31, 2000, and pitched under the name of Jairo Garcia. In the spring of 2006, it was revealed that his real name was Santiago Casilla.

Why would a baseball player with no criminal or troublesome past change his name?

Santiago Casilla was nineteen and lived in the Dominican Republic. It was there that he changed his name and became Jairo Garcia, taking the name and birth certificate of a friend nearly three years younger. For the next five seasons, Casilla lived a lie. But why? "When Americans [baseball scouts] come to the Dominican Republic, they like young guys," Casilla said. "They're not going to sign guys who are too old."

According to manager Bob Geren of the Oakland A's, Casilla is not the only one to change his name. It was an act of desperation. At the time it seemed like the only way to achieve his dream of pitching in the major leagues. MLB spokesman Pat Courtney said, "There were a number of cases. It was an issue. But after a situation like 9-11, there was an added emphasis from the State Department and others to make sure all visas and personal ID's matched up."

Secondly, Casilla later proved his worth by playing a prominent relief-pitching role in the San Francisco Giants winning the 2012 National League's divisional playoffs and advancing to the World Series. He also was the winning pitcher in Game 4 of the 2012 World Series as the San Francisco Giants swept the Detroit Tigers.

Later, Casilla made what may have been the worst at-bat appearance in baseball history. The Giants played the Florida Marlins on August 14, 2011, at Sun Life Stadium, in Miami. With the Giants beating the Marlins 5-2, San Francisco manager Bruce Bochy sent his relief pitcher, Santiago Casilla, to the plate in the top of the ninth inning. Casilla had pitched in the bottom of the eighth, and Bochy didn't want to remove him for a pointless at-bat with the team's regular closer unavailable. Casilla had never batted in the major leagues. Bochy, only interested in keeping Casilla on the mound, gave him strict orders not to swing at any pitch; the at-bat didn't matter. The only thing that did matter was that the Giants finish off the Marlins in the bottom of the ninth to end the game with a win.

Casilla stepped into the batter's box, standing as far away from home plate as possible without stepping outside of the box. It was abundantly clear that he was content to stand there and look around at things. Casilla stood upright without a hint of taking a batting stance. With the Marlins catcher's glove targeting the center of the plate, the Marlins reliever Jose Ceda's only challenge was to throw three strikes to a player who was obviously not going to swing the bat. Things didn't work out that way. Ceda did the unbelievable—he walked Casilla on four straight pitches. Casilla's episode at-bat is called by many, "The worst plate appearance in baseball history." I simply saw it as "rock bottom."

Nearly a year later, Casilla picked up his first base hit during his nine-year major league career. With bases loaded, Casilla drove in one run during the ballgame on September 14, 2012 against the Arizona Diamondbacks.

The Strangest

The best way to describe the game that took place on May 10, 2013, between the Tampa Bay Rays, playing at home against the San Diego Padres, is "weird...perplexing."

The Rays' starter, Alex Cobb, struck out every batter that he faced in the third inning, yet the Padres were able to put a run on the scoreboard. Here's what happened:

Cobb struck out Will Venable to start the third, but he unleashed a wild pitch that went to the backstop for strike three. That wild pitch allowed Venable to run and reach first base safely. Venable then stole second on the same pitch that saw Chase Headley become Cobb's second strikeout. Venable stole third shortly before Carlos Quentin became Cobb's third strikeout victim of the inning. Despite Cobb's bad luck, he appeared close to escaping the inning unscathed. Then Cobb made a "bush-league" mistake of committing a balk[8]. That balk allowed Venable to score a run. Yonder Alonso was next up, and he struck out swinging to give Cobb four strikeouts for the inning. So, there you have it. Four Padres batters went to the plate; all four struck out—yet the Padres still managed to score a run.

"Off-the-Wall" Homer

Mention Jim Piersall's name and sports buffs will likely recall the Red Sox player with a terrible temper who did a number of weird things both on and off the playing field, including getting into fights with his competitors and teammates. Doctors later discovered that Piersall suffered from manic-depressive disorder, and hospitalized him for several weeks. His story was portrayed in the non-fiction book and movie, *Fear Strikes Out.*

As a batboy in the early '50s, I spent a fair amount of time with Jim Piersall when the Boston Red Sox played the Washington Senators at Griffith Stadium. I thought Jim was one of the best defensive outfielders in the American League. While I did see Jim's temper tantrums and weird stunts on a few occasions, he was always nice to me. Some of his stunts consisted of walking up to bat wearing a Beatles wig, talking to the monument of Babe Ruth at Yankee Stadium, and climbing a grandstand roof to heckle an umpire.

Piersall made "history" for a stunt he pulled while playing for the New York Mets. The date was June 23, 1963, and the Mets were playing the Philadelphia Phillies at Connie Mack Stadium in Philadelphia. In the top of the fifth, the lead-off hitter, Jim Piersall, stepped up to the plate facing the Phillies pitcher, Dallas Green. Piersall swung and solidly connected—home run. This was not just any home run, it was career homer No. 100. Already thirty-three, Jim Piersall knew that he would never reach the 200 home runs mark. So Jim decided to celebrate this memorable milestone by running the bases in proper order, but backward. The media and fans everywhere loved it! Mets' manager, Casey Stengel, was not impressed and released Piersall two days later. The California Angels picked him up a month after that release.

Jim Piersall spent seventeen seasons in the majors and played 1,734 games. He compiled a lifetime record of hitting .272, with 104 home runs and 591 RBIs. Jim played in two All-Star games, and won two Gold Gloves. Few people remember Jim Piersall as a talented ball player. They remember him for his eccentric behavior. That behavior made Jim Piersall famous and in demand as a public speaker and TV announcer.

It's an Error...Please!

On June 17, 1942, Paul Waner of the Boston Braves had 2,999 career hits. During the game against Cincinnati at Braves Field, and in the fifth inning,

Waner hit a sharp grounder to the right of the Reds shortstop, Eddie Joost. Joost made a backhanded attempt to catch the ball, but was only able to knock it down. The scorekeeper, Jerry Moore, recorded the play on the official game scorecard as a hit.

The awarding of this "much less than impressive" hit meant that it would be documented in baseball's record books as Waner's 3,000th career hit. However, Waner waved furiously at the press box demanding that the call be changed to an error. "No, no! Don't give me a hit on that. I won't take it," Waner shouted. He waved away umpire Beans Reardon, as well as converging players, who rushed onto the field to offer their congratulations. Finally, amid all the hullabaloo, Moore changed his decision and charged Joost with an error.

Two days later, in a home game against Pittsburgh, Waner ripped a clean shot—his 3,000th hit off Pirates pitcher Rip Sewell in the fifth inning. Waner later said, "I wanted my 3,000th hit to be a clean one."

It wasn't until almost sixteen years later that another MLB player joined the select few in the 3,000-hit club. On May 13, 1958, Stan Musial of the St. Louis Cardinals became a member of this select group with a pinch-hit double off of Moe Drabowsky at Wrigley Field.

3000 Hits Club

For a player to achieve 3,000 hits and become a member of the elite 3,000 Hits Club is more of a personal plateau than an actual award. As of June 19, 2015, the 3,000 Hits Club had only twenty-nine members. Membership is only attained by those select few who have combined a consistently high level of hitting with a remarkably lengthy career. It is a benchmark that few will achieve. Most noticeably missing are a few of the greatest hitters of all time including Joe DiMaggio, Jimmie Foxx, Mickey Mantle, Babe Ruth, and Ted Williams.

Membership in this club often serves as a guarantee of eventual entry into the National Baseball Hall of Fame.

The Unsurpassed

A MLB player getting nine hits in eleven times at-bat in a single game is not only record-setting, it's unbelievable. Yet, on July 10, 1932, Johnny Burnett of the Cleveland Indians did just that in an 18-inning game against the Philadelphia Athletics. Perhaps, the best way to cite the greatness of Burnett's accomplishment would be to say that no other player has ever gotten more than seven hits in any Major League Baseball game, even those that went into extra innings.

On June 18, 1953, Gene Stephens of the Boston Red Sox became the first American League player to have three hits in the same inning. Five decades later, on June 27, 2003, Johnny Damon, also of the Red Sox, tied Stephens' three-hit record.

CHAPTER EIGHT

The Game's Biggest Blunders

"The toughest call an umpire has to make is not the half-swing; the toughest call is throwing a guy out of the game after you blew the hell out of the play."

—*Umpire Johnny Rice*

The Game's Biggest Boners...Oops, Blunders

In my last book on baseball, I took it for granted that readers would know the meaning of a pitcher's "balk" when I talked about it. A few were unfamiliar with that word, so I learned not to take things, especially the meaning of baseball jargon for granted. Therefore, you will find that I sometimes appear to interchange two specific words in this chapter. So as not to create any misunderstandings, let me say this: My definition of the word "blunder" as I use it means a careless or embarrassing physical mistake. To me, the slang word "boner" is a clumsy or stupid mental mistake. Unfortunately, Major League Baseball is filled with all sorts of blunders and a few really stupid boners. There are also those stupid mistakes or boners that were made by a team's owner, league official or Baseball Commissioner's office. However, whether it be a boner or blunder, players are generally the ones responsible.

The Players

Anytime even the most talented humans are involved in a game such as baseball that demands blinding speed and meticulous timing, moments of extreme jubilation or heartbreak are bound to occur. Such statistics and events—from the most spectacular plays to the worst blunders ever—fill the record books of baseball.

Among the literally thousands of errors or mistakes that have taken place in Major League Baseball, a few are downright funny. Then there are those that not only cost a team their championship, but left the player who committed that particular blunder or boner, mentally damaged for life. I personally witnessed one such incident. It took place at Griffith Stadium in Washington, D.C. on Friday, April 17, 1953. I was serving as batboy for the New York Yankees.

In the top of the fifth inning, Mickey Mantle stepped into the batter's box to face the Senators' southpaw, Chuck Stobbs. Mantle, a switch-hitter, was batting right-handed when Stobbs went into his delivery and served up a chest-high fastball. Mantle took a powerful swing and the ball exploded off his bat. There was no question that the ball was headed for the left-center field bleachers. However, it kept going higher and higher, glanced off the fifty-six foot *Mr. Boh* beer sign, and traveled out of the stadium. Mantle's home run was the longest ever hit in Griffith Stadium's history—a 565-foot "tape-measure" blast. Publicity about this "tape-measure" homer was enormous and this clout made the *Guinness Book of World Records*.

For the 21-year-old Mickey Mantle it was a momentous occasion. For Chuck Stobbs, it was a single, but devastating pitch. Stobbs would always be remembered for that one pitch. It didn't matter that he won 107 games during his fifteen seasons in the majors, nor that that pitch took place in only one-half inning out of 1,900 innings pitched. It was forever etched in Chuck Stobbs' mind and he carried that haunting memory to his grave. He once said, "That's one day I'd like to forget, but nobody lets me."

Baseball is filled with legends; some joyous like Mantle's, others sad like Stobbs', and a few so mind-boggling they are almost beyond belief. Here's one, and it involves a player named Smead Jolley:

According to folklore, Smead Jolley once committed three errors on a single play—that's right, three errors by one player on a single play! This story first appeared in the December 1932 issue of *Baseball Magazine*, and was told by Goose Goslin of the Washington Senators. Goose said that the Washington Senators were playing in Comiskey Park in 1930, when their batter hit a ball to Smead Jolley in the outfield. The ball rolled between Jolly's legs, bounced off the wall behind him, shooting backward between Jolley's legs, as it moved in the opposite direction. When Jolley finally retrieved the ball, he threw toward third as the batter streaked around the bases headed for third base. However, Jolley's throw was way off target; the ball sailed into the stands.

A similar story by Russell Schneider, a Cleveland sports writer, puts the three-error play as taking place during a game at Cleveland's League Park. This particular story was allegedly told to Schneider by pitcher Mel Harder, as he recalled the incident, naming Glenn Myatt as the batter. Still another story places Jolley's triple-error incident as taking place in Philadelphia's Shibe Park. This story is basically the same as those above, except for the ballpark, and naming Bing Miller as the batter.

Differing versions of this story "took legs" and appeared in various news-papers, including a May 17, 1946, article in the *New York Times*, one in the *Washington Post* on January 28, 1962, and still another in the *San Francisco Examiner* on February 1, 1976. Similar stories can also be found in various baseball books including *The Baseball Hall of Shame; Baseball Players and Their Times: Oral Histories of the Game, 1920-1940*; and *The Cleveland Indians Encyclopedia*.

Here's what I know about Smead Jolley: On November 4, 1929, the Chicago White Sox signed Jolley. Ten days later (November 14, 1929), the *Sporting News* ran a story about Jolley on its front page, and dubbed him the "Arkansas Assassin" with a comparison to Babe Ruth, in that both began as pitchers and both were powerful left-handed hitters.

Smead Jolley made his first official error in a game against the Red Sox while playing at Fenway Park, Boston. With two outs, the Sox's Tom Oliver singled to right field. Jolly, running at top speed, completely missed fielding the ball as he overran it. By the time Jolly retrieved the ball, two runs had scored, and the batter, Tom Oliver, ended up on third. The Red Sox went on to win the game, 3-1.

Career-wise, Smead Jolley compiled a .305 lifetime batting average and had considerable power. As an outfielder in the majors, he made 44 errors in 418 games.

Smead Jolley died of a stroke on November 17, 1991, while at the South Shore Convalescent Hospital in Alameda, CA. His ashes were scattered in the Pacific Ocean, three miles west of the Golden Gate Bridge.

Those outlandish tales about Smead Jolly's triple-error taking place on a single play are highly questionable. According to SABR.org, "a perusal of box scores on Retrosheet[9] during Smead Jolly's entire major-league career shows no game in which Jolley was ever charged with two errors in the same game." The SABR site confirmed that Smead Jolly did commit 44 errors in 418 games, and that he had a career major-league fielding percentage of .946.

My take: A funny and attention-getting yarn, but unlikely to be true.

Bill Buckner's Blunder — October 25, 1986

Few errors prove more costly than those made in a World Series or Pennant race. Boston Red Sox first baseman, Bill Buckner, learned a devastating life lesson during the early morning hours of October 26, 1986, when he failed to field an easy ground ball in the 1986 World Series. Here's how it went down:

With a comfortable 5-3 lead in the bottom of the tenth inning in Game 6 (leading the series 3-2), Boston allowed the Mets to tie the game. Mookie Wilson came to the plate. On the tenth pitch of the at-bat, after fouling off six pitches, Wilson poked an easy ground ball to Buckner at first base. It looked like the game would go to the eleventh inning, but Buckner (playing with both ankles injured) misplayed the ball and it rolled between his legs and down the right-field line as Ray Knight bolted home from second base to score the game-winning run. With that unbelievable 6-5 win, the Series was now tied at three games each. Two nights later in Game 7, Boston's bad luck continued. They lost their 3-0 lead in the sixth inning when the Mets tied the game. In the seventh, the Mets scored another three runs, and with that the New York Mets went on to win the 1986 World Series championship.

Bill Buckner discovered—in the cruelest way possible—one play can define a career. That costly error overshadowed the remainder of his career. Buckner began receiving death threats, and was heckled and booed by some of his home team's fans. Meanwhile, he was the focal point of derision from the fans of opposing teams on the road — especially when he faced the Mets in Spring training 1987, and the first time he came to bat at Yankee Stadium during the regular season.

The Red Sox released Buckner on July 23, 1987. As his career was winding down, he joined the California Angels and later the Kansas City Royals. In April 1990, he briefly returned to the Red Sox as a free agent and retired on June 5th. On April 8, 2008, Buckner threw out the first pitch at the Red Sox home opener. He received a four-minute ovation from the sell-out crowd. After the game, when Buckner was asked if he had any second thoughts about appearing at the game, he said, "I really had to forgive, not the fans of Boston, per se, but…I would have to say in my heart I had to forgive the media for what they put me and my family through. So, you know, I've done that and I'm over that."

Fred Snodgrass' Muff — October 16, 1912

Game 7 in a World Series is one of the most awesome events in sports. But if reaching the seventh game is amazing, how much more exciting is eight? That's right…eight!

In 1912, the Boston Red Sox and New York Giants actually played eight games in that year's World Series, because Game 2 was called a tie after the eleventh inning because of darkness. The location of this final and deciding Game 8 was determined by a coin flip, which the Red Sox won. Because this game was scheduled at the last minute, Wednesday, October 16th was the date selected for play in Boston's Fenway Park. It was in this rare eighth game that Fred Snodgrass would commit one of the most famous blunders in baseball history. Here is how it happened:

With the two teams tied 1-1 at the end of the ninth, play moved into extra innings. In the top of the tenth, the Giants pulled ahead by one run. When the Red Sox came to bat in the bottom half of the tenth inning, the Giants were leading 2-1. First to bat for the Sox was pinch hitter, Clyde Engle. Engle, batting in place of pitcher Joe Wood, lofted an easy fly ball to right center field. Center fielder Fred Snodgrass moved into position and called for it. The ball landed in Snodgrass' glove, but bounced out and fell to the ground. On that blunder, Engle was able to reach second base. Boston's next batter, Harry Hooper, stepped up to the plate and drilled a long shot that Snodgrass speared for a spectacular running catch. Engle, expecting the ball to drop safely, took off from second, bound for home, running the base path at full speed when the ball was caught. This unexpected catch forced Engle to quickly return to second to avoid a double play. Steve Yerkes took his position at the plate, and was walked by the Giants' pitcher, Christy Mathewson. With Yerkes' walk, the winning run for the Red Sox was now on base, and Tris Speaker, Boston's best hitter, was next to bat.

Then another blunder happened: Mathewson got Speaker to hit an easy foul popup on the first base side. The first baseman (Fred Merkle), catcher (Chief Meyers) and pitcher (Christy Mathewson), all converged on that popup. Though most spectators agreed Merkle should have been the one to catch the ball, he stepped aside when Mathewson called for Chief Meyers to make the catch. However, Meyers was not close enough to reach the ball. It fell to the ground untouched between the three men. Given another chance at-bat, Speaker rapped a single that scored Engle, and with that run crossing the plate, the game was tied. Lewis was the next batter.

Giants manager, McGraw, signaled an intentional pass be given to Duffy Lewis. His thinking was to load the bases, and create an opportunity for a force-out at any base. However, McGraw's plan didn't work. Larry Gardner's sacrifice fly brought Yerkes home with the winning run and Boston won the World Series.

Fred Snodgrass' "$30,000 muff" (the payout to be divided between the losers and winners of the series was $29,514) became a legendary part of baseball's history.

In 1915, after eight seasons with the Giants, Snodgrass was sold to the Boston Braves. He finished his major league career with the Braves a year later. Snodgrass' nine-year lifetime batting average was .275 with 351 RBIs and 215 stolen bases in 923 games. He moved to California, spent 1917 in the Pacific Coast League and later retired to go into the appliance business.

In 1940, Fred Snodgrass said, "Hardly a day in my life, hardly an hour, that in some manner or other the dropping of that fly doesn't come up, even after 30 years. On the street, in my store, at my home...it's all the same. They might choke up before they ask me and they hesitate–but they always ask."

In his book, *My Thirty Years in the Game*, Giants manager John McGraw remarked, "Often I have been asked what I did to Fred Snodgrass after he dropped that fly ball in the World Series of 1912...I will tell you exactly what I did: I raised his salary $1,000."

Fred Snodgrass took the blame for the Giants' loss even though the biggest mistake of the inning was the misplay on Speaker's foul ball for which Mathewson is to blame. In situations such as this, it is the pitcher's (Mathewson) responsibility to call for a fielder to take the pop up. Merkle should have been the one designated to make the catch.

The New York Times article on the game carried the banner headlines:

"SOX CHAMPIONS ON MUFFED FLY"

"SNODGRASS DROPS EASY BALL, COSTING TEAMMATES $29,514"

The Times' article lead with these words: "Write in the pages of world series baseball history the name of Snodgrass. Write it large and black. Not as hero; truly not."

Despite his solid contributions to three pennant-winning clubs, Fred Snodgrass will forever be remembered for his infamous "$30,000 muff" in the final game of the 1912 World Series. When Snodgrass died on April 5, 1974, his obituary in *The New York Times* was headlined "Fred Snodgrass, 86, Dead; Ball Player Muffed 1912 Fly."

Mickey Owen's Muff

Mickey Owen is recognized as one of the best defensive catchers in the history of Major League Baseball. Unfortunately, during the 1926 W.S. he became linked with other outstanding players, such as Fred Merkle, Ralph Branca, and Bill Buckner; all defined by a single moment of bad luck in baseball's history books.

The date was October 5, 1941. The setting—ninth inning of Game 4 of the World Series at Ebbets Field. The Yankees trailed the Brooklyn Dodgers 4-3 with two outs. Tommy Henrich was at the plate, facing Dodgers ace reliever Hugh Casey. With nobody on base and a full count on Henrich, Casey delivered a sharply breaking pitch. Henrich swung at the ball and missed. The home-plate umpire, Larry Goetz, signaled a strikeout, thus appearing to end the game.

However, the pitched ball hit the heel of Mickey Owen's mitt and hopped away. With the "passed ball" rule in effect, Owen chased the ball near the Dodgers' dugout, Henrich ran to first base. Joe DiMaggio followed with a single to left, and then Charlie Keller hit a ball high off the right-field screen, scoring both Henrich and DiMaggio and giving the Yankees a 5-4 lead. Bill Dickey walked, Joe Gordon doubled, increasing the score to 7-4. The Dodgers went down quickly in the bottom of the ninth, and with this miraculous win, the Yankees took a three game to one

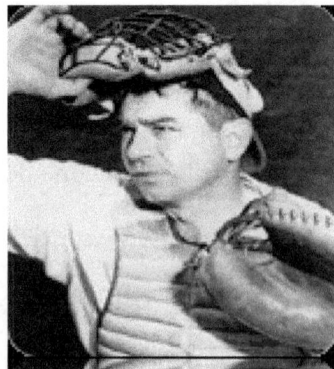

lead in the series. The following day, the Yankees won and became the World Series champions.

In 1999, Mickey Owen's son, Charlie Owen, told the Toronto Star that his father said, "it was a combination of a wild pitch, a wild swing, a catcher's muff, and an overzealous Dodgers' fan who tried to kick the ball back to him and missed."

Whatever the reason, Mickey Owen's dropped third strike error in Game 4 of the 1941 World Series, became recognized as one of the game's most embarrassing moments for a player.

"The Babe's" Biggest Blunder?

As discussed in Chapter Two, with the 1926 World Series between the New York Yankees and St. Louis Cardinals tied at three games apiece, Game 7— the final and series deciding game—was to be played at Yankee Stadium on Sunday afternoon, October 10th.

Each of the two teams were considered to be strong both offensively and defensively, but the Yankees remained heavy favorites, primarily because of their "Murderers Row" lineup consisting of Earle Combs, Mark Koenig, Babe Ruth, Bob Meusel, Lou Gehrig and Tony Lazzeri.

With the Cardinals leading 3-2 in the bottom of the ninth, Babe Ruth stepped up to the plate. "The Babe" worked the count to three and two, then drew what would be his eleventh walk of the series. Cleanup hitter, Bob Meusel, who closed out the season with a .315 batting average, was now at-bat. Lou Gehrig, a .358 hitter in this series, was waiting in the on-deck circle. However, Meusel would never get a chance to exhibit his hitting prowess because Ruth broke for second in an attempted steal. The Cards catcher Bob O'Farrell's rifle throw to Rogers Hornsby was on target and nailed the Yankee slugger as he slid into second base for the third final out of the game. "The Babe's" unbelievable blunder gave the World Series championship to the St. Louis Cardinals.

Was Babe Ruth's attempted steal really a boner?

Father Gabe Costa's well-researched article that was published in the *CBS Newsletter* dated July 29, 2011, offered the following for consideration before rendering your judgment:

"With Ruth now on first and representing the tying run, the cleanup batter Bob Meusel stepped up to hit. In Game 6, Babe Ruth had successfully stolen second base against the very same pitcher (Alexander) and catcher (Bob O'Farrell). According to reports, his steal was rather easy, and this would be the only stolen base for the Yankees during this entire series.

Babe Ruth was no slacker when it came to stealing bases. Career-wise, he had stolen 123 bases, plus another four in World Series games, led the Yankees in stolen bases in 1920, with fourteen, and in 1923, with seventeen. However, that same year, he was caught attempting to steal twenty-one times, which is poor by any standards. In 1921, he shared the team lead with Meusel, again with fourteen. As the slugging outfielder with the Yankees, Ruth successfully racked up 110 stolen bases; while with the Boston Red Sox as a pitcher-outfielder, he successfully stole thirteen bases. However, few will argue that Babe Ruth ran bases too aggressively. His career stolen base totals calculate to a fifty-five percent success rate. However, the data kept on stolen bases appear full of errors. Unfortunately, baseball fans everywhere expect statistics to be accurate, especially for premier players such as Babe Ruth. The American League didn't start reliably keeping caught-stealing records until 1920 and the National League not until 1951. Those stats reported above may or may not be valid.

As Ruth noted in his autobiography, he had the element of surprise in his favor; Alexander admitted that he "forgot all about Ruth" on first.

Hall of Fame umpire Billy Evans wrote in his nationally syndicated column (*Toledo News Bee*, October 20, 1926) that "Babe was out on a hair-line decision." Evans also went on to say that what Ruth did was "perfectly proper baseball.

The fact that he failed in his objective means nothing as to the correctness of the play…the odds were all against Meusel getting an extra-base hit."

By the time Bob Meusel came to bat with Babe Ruth on first base in the ninth inning of Game Seven, he was hitting .238 (5 for 21) for the series, and had not knocked in a solitary run. (It is fair to say that he had not delivered a single key hit. Perhaps even worse, Bob had misplayed two balls during the Cardinals' three-run fourth inning rally, including the dropping of a routine fly.)

Speculation was that Ruth just didn't think that his old companion Meusel had any realistic chance of driving him in from first base against Grover Cleveland Alexander.

Catcher Bob O'Farrell's throw to Rogers Hornsby was perfectly executed and it nailed the Yankees' slugger ending the Fall Classic.

Rogers Hornsby later recalled, "Ruth didn't say a word. He didn't even look around or up at me. He just picked himself up and walked away." Many of those fans attending the game were furious with Ruth and believed that his mistake had clearly cost the series.

Near the end of this extensive article, Father Costa added, "It has been approximately four years since I wrote my book about Babe Ruth trying to steal second base in the 1926 World Series. In the interim, after researching the matter even further, I have become more convinced that the controversial incident displayed Babe Ruth at his absolute best. I wrote:

Along with extraordinary natural ability, athletic courage was the essence of Ruth's greatness… Babe relentlessly pursued victory and greatness, and never let fear of failure or ridicule deter him…if Ruth had not tried to steal that base, the Yankees chances of winning would have been reduced. If he hadn't possessed the guts to take the chance, Babe Ruth would not have become the game's greatest player.

I am comfortable with having said that. Ruth's literal transcendence as a baseball player was due to his irrestrainable interaction of body, mind and spirit. It was that quintessential blend of rare qualities that rendered him unique. Only Babe Ruth possessed the spontaneous athletic wisdom and total absence of fear to have dared to do what he did. I regard the ending of the 1926 World Series as a highlight of Babe Ruth's career as well as one of the shining moments in the annals of America's sports culture."

CHAPTER NINE
Unbelievably Raw Deal

"Won't they ever stop?"
—*Fred Merkle*

As Fred Merkle's family had done for years, they nearly always attended their Florida church on Sunday mornings to listen to their minister's teachings of the gospel. To the family, this particular 1930s Sunday would be no different from others... or so they thought.

The family entered the church, took their seats and waited for the service to begin. Promptly at 9:00 A.M. their minister stepped forward and announced that a visiting minister would deliver that morning's message. Walking to the pulpit, the guest minister chuckled as he declared, "I want to begin by admitting to you an ugly secret. I am from Toledo, Ohio—birthplace of the infamous Fred 'Bonehead' Merkle." With that introduction, Fred Merkle silently stood up, and led his family out the door.

"Bonehead" had heard that cruel word hundreds, if not thousands, of times. As he and his family headed home, Fred silently wondered, "Won't they ever stop?"

Fred Merkle certainly was not a bonehead, nor a quitter! Yet, he could not escape the haunting memory of that one play...a misstep that nearly destroyed his Major League Baseball career, and agonizingly consumed a huge portion of his personal life.

The date was September 23, 1908. The Chicago Cubs were playing the New York Giants. The two teams were locked in a red-hot pennant race with only fifteen more games left in the '08 season.

Giants manager John McGraw greeted Merkle with some exciting news when he arrived at the ballpark. Merkle would be starting at first base, as regular first baseman Fred Tenney was out with a back injury. This was the only game Tenney had missed all season, and conversely, the only game Merkle started.

As the game progressed, it became a classic pitchers' duel between the Giants legendary pitcher Christy Mathewson and Cubs Jack Pfiester. The two teams were tied 1-1, as the game moved into the bottom of the ninth. With two outs, the Giants Moose McCormick singled and held up at first. Fred Merkle stepped into the batter's box and launched a long single into the right field corner—his first of the game. Giants' fans roared. The 19-year-old rookie was thrilled beyond belief. McCormick scurried from first to third base, putting himself in an easy scoring position. Not wanting to take any chances on being nailed at second, Merkle made the turn, hesitated, and returned to first base.

The next batter, shortstop Al Bridwell, stepped to the plate. The pitcher, Jack Pfiester, going into his delivery stretch, eyed Merkle who had taken somewhat of risky lead off first. Bridwell, seeing their eye-ball-to-eye-ball exchange between the two, feared that Merkle could be picked-off for the third out. Bridwell stepped out of the box and signaled Merkle to reduce the length of his risky lead. Back in the box and ready, Pfiester delivered. Bridwell swung and sent a blazing line drive straight up the middle, causing the base umpire, Bob Emslie, to hit the ground to avoid being hit. At the same time, McCormick, hands clapping, trotted across the plate racking up the game-winning run.

Seeing McCormick score, Merkle thought the game was over, and commenced to jump up and down in celebration. Many of the Giants' fans, also caught up in the thrill of their home team's conquest over the Cubs, went into a wild frenzy, as they poured onto the field. Swarming the field at game's end was nothing new at the Polo Grounds. The most convenient way out of the park was to cross the diamond and exit via the center field gates. Recognizing the safety risks involved as an uncontrollable mob approached, Merkle did what other players generally did during those days. He made a beeline for his team's clubhouse in center field, to avoid the swarm of crazed Giants' fans as they rushed wildly onto the field.

To practically everyone in attendance, the game was over—a huge win for the Giants. Wait, hold on! The alert Cubs shortstop, Johnny Evers, saw Merkle leave the base path before he touched second base. Evers, a rules' scholar, was confident that Merkle had violated Rule 59. To him, this game was far from over. He had to get his hands on the ball and quickly step on second base to validate out number three; thus nullifying the Giants' "winning" run.

Competing with the near deafening noise of the crowd, Evers began screaming and waving to get the attention of his center fielder, Solly Hofman. Hofman, who had fielded Bridwell's hit—thinking the game over—had started to leisurely trot from the field, ball in hand.

Evers' shouting and odd aerobics caught the attention of a couple of team-mates—the message was clear: get the ball to second base. With renewed excitement, they each began to shout for Hofman to get the ball back into the infield. Hofman suddenly understood the urgency! Shifting from a slow trot to a running pace, Hofman rocketed the ball in the direction of second base, well off target. It flew over Evers' head, hitting the Cubs shortstop, Joe Tinker, in the back.

The accuracy of what took place from this point on is lost in time, and sub-ject to much controversy. The next day's newspapers contained at least a half dozen drastically different versions of what actually took place at the apparent end of the game. Some accounts say the ball, after flying over Evers' head, ended up in the hands of Giants coach Joe McGinnity, who, having seen what was about to transpire, threw the ball deep into the stands to prevent the play from taking place. Others tell stories of Cubs pitcher Rube Kroh punching and taking the ball away from a New York fan, then tossing it to Johnny Evers, who stepped on second base. A couple others say that Evers, after seeing McGinnity fling the ball into the stands was yelling that if the ball was gone, he wanted another one. Still there are those who argued another ball was somehow given to Evers by either Harry Steinfeldt or Joe Tinker.

Whatever the ball's origin—official game ball or substituted ball—Evers stepped on second base with that ball in hand. He turned to umpire Bob Emslie, and appealed for the third out to be called based on Merkle's violation of Rule 59. Emslie refused. Emslie claimed he did not see the play because Bridwell's blazing line drive caused him to hit the ground. Home plate umpire Hank O'Day said he saw what happened at second, and would take responsi-bility for determining whether or not a violation of Rule 59 had occurred.

*Rule 59, (now Rule 4.09 a.) states: One run shall be scored each time a runner legally advances to and touches first, second, third and home base before three men are put out to end the inning. EXCEPTION: **A run is not scored if the runner advances to home base during a play in which the third out is made** (1) by the batter-runner before he touches first base; (2) by any runner being forced out; or (3) by a preceding runner who is declared out because he failed to touch one of the bases.*

No wonder the events that took place in this game became so debatable. Even the proper enforcement of Rule 59 was a controversial issue. It was a known fact that Rule 59 was rarely enforced. In fact, one of the more vocal critics, the editor for *The Sporting Life*, a weekly newspaper, went on record saying, "Merkle only did what has been done in hundreds of championship games in the major leagues, and what has been done a hundred times this year in such games."

To further arouse suspicion that Evers' claim was possibly invalid, it was pointed out that Johnny Evers used a similar situation a few days earlier (September 4th) in a Cubs game against the Pittsburgh Pirates. That score was tied at "0" when it went into extra innings. In the bottom of the tenth inning, the Pirates had the bases loaded. Pirates batter, Chief Wilson, punched a two-out single that scored the winning run. Johnny Evers claimed rookie Warren Gill, the runner on first, didn't touch second base. Upon seeing Gill leave the diamond, Evers yelled for the ball, retrieved it, and stomped his foot on the bag. Evers screamed at the umpire, Hank O'Day that the Pittsburg player was out when he (Gill) failed to touch second. O'Day, tired of Evers' persistent challenges, snapped that the game was over and the Pirates had won. The crafty veteran Evers—a stickler for rules—became livid and continued to argue that the base-runner's failure to touch second was a rule's violation and should have been ruled an out. Evers made it a point to make certain that the umpire, Hank O'Day, would not forget in the future. He convinced the Cubs' owner, to file an official appeal with the National League claiming that an official rule (Rule 59) had been ignored. The appeal was denied.

What does that September 4th game between the Cubs and Pirates have to do with the September 23rd game? Plenty—the same team (Cubs); same fielder (Evers); same umpire (O'Day); and the circumstances were nearly identical.

Now let us rejoin the September 23rd game:

After a long delay O'Day emerged from a conference with Emslie to rule that Merkle was out, thus nullifying the Giants winning run. Despite the umpire's ruling, the game was unable to proceed because of the huge number of uncontrollable fans on the field. The game was declared a 1-1 tie to be replayed at a later time, if necessary. Giants manager, John McGraw, was incensed at the ruling and appealed to National League president, Harry Pulliam.

The next morning, Merkle found that his nightmare had grown even worse...splashed all over the morning newspapers were headlines with hurtful comments blaming him for the loss. *The New York Times* blamed the loss on "censurable stupidity on the part of player Merkle." Another newspaper cited the stupidity of Fred Merkle, and still others labeled him "Bonehead."

On the heels of those negative newspaper articles, McGraw received an answer from the League's president. No surprise. McGraw had been fined and suspended several times by Pulliam for umpire abuse, so, as expected, Pulliam upheld his umpire's ruling. However, it was decided that if the two teams ended the season tied in the standings, a replay of the "Merkle" game would be necessary. (A rematch became necessary, and that game was played on October 8th. The Cubs won 4-2 and went on to win the 1908 World Series.)

The Merkle controversy continued. Fred Merkle, only nineteen at the time, was vilified by both fans and the news media. Back then, the *Sporting News*, the game's official Bible, published an article about "the stupidity of Fred Merkle." Everywhere newspapers labeled him "Bonehead." Others blamed Giants manager John McGraw for setting the stage for the "boner" to occur, holding him responsible for not ensuring that his team was made aware of what Evers pulled in the widely publicized September 4th game between the Cubs and Pirates.

According to Fred Merkle's own affidavit, he was about 15 feet from second base when he veered towards the clubhouse. Chicago's center fielder, Artie Hofman had fielded Bridwell's hit and thrown the ball towards second-baseman Johnny Evers, but somehow Giants coach Joe McGinnity came up with the ball and lobbed it deep into the crowd. While Evers was trying to recover Hofman's throw, Merkle, once he became aware of what was happening, claimed he returned to second base and stood there while the Cubs protested. He remained there until Christy Mathewson came along and said, "Come on, let's go to the clubhouse. Emslie [umpire] said he would not allow the claim."

"Merkle was careless, to be sure," wrote *Baseball Magazine*, "but withal, he did only what many others had done without suffering criticism."

Fred Merkle was recognized as an intelligent, shrewd, and aggressive player, who packed a wallop at the plate in the days of the "dead" ball. His batting average was always close to the .300 mark. In 1912, he hit .309. Fred retired from baseball in 1927 and moved to Florida, where he lived a quiet life with his family. Those who knew him described Fred Merkle as a man of intelligence and courage, who was quiet but competitive and determined to do his best at all times. Yet, the haunting "Bonehead" label couldn't be shaken. He stayed clear of the MLB spotlight until one day in 1950. At the urging of his daughter, the sixty-one-year old Merkle accepted an invitation from New York Giants president Horace Stoneman to be a guest at an old-timers game on July 30, 1950. He did so with hesitation. How would the crowd react to him after all those years? Would he once again have to listen to "Bonehead" chants? No! The Giants fans cheered loudly, and gave Fred Merkle, a most welcomed...ovation.

During an interview in 1955, within one year of his death, Fred was asked about the play. "It has never been a pleasant subject for me to discuss," he said. "For years while I continued to play, it haunted me and kept me in constant fear of what can happen to me now."

Prior to his death, Fred was so concerned that some prankster would inscribe "Bonehead" on his headstone; he left instructions for his grave to be left unmarked. Fred Merkle died at his home in Daytona Beach, Florida, on March 2, 1956. His obituary read, "Bonehead play goes to grave with Fred Merkle."

In 2005, his family and friends erected a beautiful memorial for him on the grounds of the Octagon House, in Watertown, Wisconsin, the town of his birth.

Fred Merkle was forever tormented by his mistake, that single play. For years, it was as if nothing else mattered to disrespectful baseball fans and vicious newspaper reporters, other than to continue to ridicule Fred Merkle. It

didn't matter that in 1908, the New York Giants would lose six more games after the game that destroyed Fred Merkle.

Bottom line, this game has become the most controversial topic of any ever played in Major League Baseball; its events have been, and will be, argued forever. Unfortunately, there will never be any universally accepted version of what actually took place during that September 23, 1908 meeting between the New York Giants and the Chicago Cubs.

That's baseball!

CHAPTER TEN

Outfielders' Greatest Defensive Plays

"Baseball is the only sport where the team on defense has the ball."

—Ken Harrelson

Wow...What a Catch!

More often than not, when a fan is talking about something exciting that happened in a game, the focus is on a mammoth home run or an outstanding pitching performance. Seldom do we hear about those dazzling catches. Yet some of the most exciting plays in the history of baseball have taken place on the defensive side of the ball field—a diving catch, one over the shoulder, or an awesome over the wall reaching catch that robbed the batter of a home run.

Spectacular catches are not officially compared against others to determine the best-of-the-best. There are simply those we remember, and those having the greatest impact on our emotions and intellect. During the regular season, it is not uncommon to see a few sensational plays that could literally take our breath away. As terrific as those catches may be, they lack the luster and impact of those made in an All-Star Game, a game that decides a league championship, or the World Series.

The Catch

If you are a baseball fan, these two words, *The Catch*, say it all! If you aren't, let me tell you about a single play that has become one of the game's most iconic moments—yes, it even ranks up there with Babe Ruth's legendary "Called Shot" in the 1932 World Series.

The Catch took place on September 29, 1954, during Game 1 of the 1954 World Series between the New York Giants and the Cleveland Indians at the Polo Grounds in New York. With the score tied, 2-2, in the top of the eighth inning, the Indians put their first two runners on base. The Giants pitcher Sal Maglie had allowed only seven hits. However, next up was the Indians first baseman Vic Wertz. Wertz had three of those seven hits; a triple and two singles. For that reason, Durocher brought in left-hander Don Liddle to face the left-hand-ed-swinging Wertz. Once the count reached two balls and one strike, Liddle delivered a shoulder-high fastball. Wertz connected and drove a solid fly ball more than 400 feet to deep

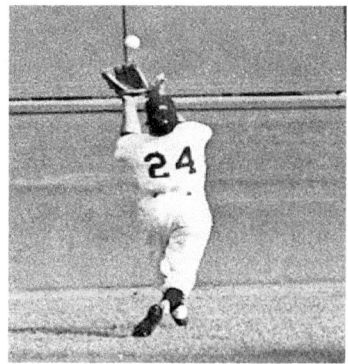

center field. In many ballparks that well hit ball would have been a home run and given the Indians a 5-2 lead. However, the Polo Grounds was larger than average. The Giants center fielder Willie Mays, playing in shallow center field, made an on-the-run, over-the-shoulder catch—similar to a football receiver taking a long pass from his quarterback—on the warning track to make the out. Having caught the ball[10], Mays immediately spun and fired the ball back to the infield. Larry Doby, the Indians runner on second, in an attempt to bring the go-ahead run across the plate took off running the moment the ball was hit. Once the catch was made, Doby hustled back to second, retagged and held up at third base. Al Rosen, taking no chances returned to first base. Liddle was relieved on the mound by Marv Grissom. The next batter walked to load the bases. However, Grissom struck out the following two batters to end the inning with no runs scored. The Giants eventually won the game 5-2 on Dusty Rhodes' pinch-hit, three-run homer in the tenth inning. The Giants went on to win the World Series in four straight games.

Named the National League's MVP in 1954, and again in 1965, Willie Mays played in a record 24 All-Star games, winning the All-Star MVP in 1963 and 1968, and was elected to the Baseball Hall of Fame in 1979.

Many fans believe that the catch made by Willie Mays in Game 1 of the 1954 World Series, later anointed as *The Catch* was the greatest ever.

But… The Greatest?

Other observers have noted that Mays' quick relay throw from deep center field was the most important part of the 1954 play, the catch itself being merely a matter of Mays outrunning the ball. In fact, Mays himself never believed it was his greatest play, much less the greatest in baseball history. In 2007, in *Ernie Hartwell's Audio Scrapbook*, Mays talked about a running bare-handed catch he made at Forbes Field in 1951, being better.

I personally have witnessed some catches that I consider more outstanding than Mays' 1954 catch. I remember seeing Boston Red Sox center fielder Jim Piersall, who was running full speed with his back to home plate, make a perfectly timed leap, turn in mid-air, and snag the ball. Unbelievable. That catch was every bit as great as the famous one made by Willie Mays. The difference was that Piersall made his incredible catch during a regular season's game in 1953 against the Washington Senators. Mays' spectacular catch took place in the 1954 World Series.

Great catches are such a subjective matter, that I seriously doubt if any single catch can be accurately labeled the finest ever. But here are a few of my greatest[11] favorites:

Kevin Mitchell

On April 26, 1989, this San Francisco Giants outfielder—chasing a ball hit off the bat of Cardinals Ozzie Smith—made a full speed dash towards the left field foul line in Busch Stadium in St. Louis when he realized he had overrun the ball. Mitchell reached back and caught the ball...barehanded[12]!

That year, the National League voted Mitchell its most valuable player. He finished his career in 1998 with 234 home runs and a .284 batting average. The only player in Major League Baseball history to win a MVP award and play for five major league teams before his thirty-second birthday. Mitchell is also the only MVP award winner to play for eight major league teams in his career.

Ron Swoboda

In 1969, the "Amazin' Mets" (a nickname coined by Casey Stengel) managed to make it all the way to the World Series to meet the American League's Baltimore Orioles, but it wasn't because of Ron Swoboda's defensive play. The outfielder was a reliable batter, but any pop fly hit in his direction was not an automatic out. In the 1969 World Series, Ron Swoboda batted fifteen times and collected six hits: one in Game 1, three in Game 4, two in Game 5—the most of any player from either team. Yet the play for which Swoboda is best remembered took place on the field in Shea Stadium on October 15th during Game 4.

It's the top of the ninth. Mets pitcher, Tom Seaver (a twenty-five-game winner) had held the Orioles scoreless through eight innings. With the Mets in front 1-0, going into the top of the ninth, Frank Robinson and Boog Powell connect with singles. With one out and runners on first and third, Brooks Robinson hits a line drive to right center; Swoboda races for the ball and makes a spectacular diving backhanded catch[13] as he descends flat-out to his right. Frank Robinson

tags up after the catch and scores, but Swoboda's superb catch prevents the go-ahead run for the Orioles from scoring.

In the bottom of the tenth inning, Jerry Grote hit a double and was replaced by pinch-runner Rod Gaspar. With the winning run on second, the Mets sent their pinch-hitter, J.C. Martin to the plate. Martin bunted. The Orioles' pitcher, Pete Richert, cleanly fielded Martin's sacrifice bunt, but his throw to first base hit Martin in the back and the ball bounced away; allowing the winning run to score. The Mets went on to take the Series in Game 5. Ron Swoboda drove in the winning run.

Baseball Weekly ranked Ron Swoboda's catch as one of the "10 Most Amazing Plays of All-Time."

Junior's Superlative Theft

The action got underway on April 26, 1990, with the Seattle Mariners playing the New York Yankees in Yankee Stadium. On the mound for Seattle was fastball pitcher Randy Johnson facing Yankees Jesse Barfield. Barfield was eager to hit his 200th career home run. Johnson delivered his fastball pitch and Barfield connected. The ball rocketed off the bat headed to left-center field, destined to become Barfield's 200th career home run. But Ken Griffey Jr. ran a country mile in Yankee Stadium's former "Death Valley," climbed the wall, and closed his glove around the ball. But it was not clear until he returned to Earth, took the ball out of his glove[14], and held it up for the world to see that he had robbed Jesse Barfield of his 200th home run. Griffey's spectacular catch was the third out of the inning and he sprinted gleefully off the field, flashing his familiar grin.

The Great Home Run Robbery

On July 1, 2006, during an interleague match between the Texas Rangers and their rival Houston Astros, Mike Lamb of the Astros hit the ball deep to centerfield. Anything short of a home run was improbable, but Gary Matthews made a tremendous vertical leap, reaching over the eight-foot wall and came away with the snag.

This catch[15] was so outstanding that Lamb himself applauded after the play was over. Team radio announcer, Eric Nadel, said it was the best catch he's ever seen a Rangers outfielder make in his 26 years with the ballclub.

Tipping of the Cap

How many times have you seen a major leaguer tip his cap to acknowledge a great catch made by a defensive player robbing him of a grand slam home run?

Here's a play that shows both an outstanding catch and a true display of sportsmanship: In the game between the Chicago Cubs and the Milwaukee Brewers, on April 12, 2009, the Cubs right fielder Milton Bradley suffered a groin strain in the bottom of the fourth inning and was replaced by Reed Johnson.

In the bottom of the fifth; Brewers Prince Fielder was at-bat facing pitcher Ryan Dempster. The bases were loaded with no outs. Fielder hit a towering, long fly ball over the head of right fielder Reed Johnson. Johnson sprinted to the wall and with a well-timed leap, scaled the eight foot wall and made a sensational catch[16]—robbing Prince Fielder of a bases-loaded grand-slam home run. As Fielder left the field, he tipped his batting helmet to Johnson.

Of the play, Fielder said, "It was a great play, You can't be mad. I did everything I was supposed to do and he did everything he was supposed to do. I guess he was just a better guy today." The Cubs went on to win the game 8-5 over the Brewers.

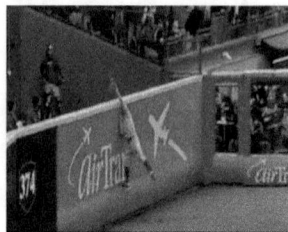

CHAPTER ELEVEN

Wacky Catches & Pitches

*"Baseball is a game where a curve is an optical illusion,
a screwball can be a pitch or a person, stealing is legal, and you
can spit anywhere you like except in the umpire's eye or on the ball."*

—*Jim Murray, sportswriter*

*Baseball players have attempted a number of wacky stunts, such as dropping
baseballs from various heights, including the Washington Monument and airplanes.*

Wacky "Away-From-Ballpark" Catches

People will do almost anything on a dare or to break an existing record, no matter what that record might be. Major League Baseball players are no different. They have done a number of wacky things off-season, or when they were not on the field. So wacky that in 2014: one of the best pitchers in baseball had to go on the disabled list; he injured himself trying to make a fancy sandwich. So wacky that a MLB manager made up an actual starting lineup for his team based on an old Tommy Tutone song.

One of the wackiest things around had to have been the stunt of a ballplayer or another person catching a baseball dropped from a great height. Speculation often focused on the Washington Monument since its construction was completed in 1884. In the late 1800s, a number of curious bar-hopping baseball fans fanned the fires of challenge, and saw the Washington Monument—with its official height of 555 feet, 5-1/8 inches—as a favorite place for anyone daring enough to test their skills at catching a baseball dropped from that height.

In 1885, just prior to the monument's dedication, Paul Hines, an outfielder for the Providence Grays, said he would give the monument challenge a try. The *New York Clipper* reported: "Hines would probably prefer to stop a pistol ball when it was coming down, hurtful as it would be to his hand, than to interfere with it when it left the barrel. It would be a good idea for Hines to first practice both ways with the pistol ball. If he likes it, he will certainly enjoy the baseball which, by the time he can see it, will be coming at a 'stand-from-under' gait of 140-ft. a second. It will not weigh much when it starts on its journey, but, great Scott, there is a rule of natural philosophy that will tell Hines before he begins just how many dozens of pounds it practically will weigh when it lands on his sconce, in case he fails to judge it correctly. Ironically, Hines was never considered to be a very good defensive outfielder. A week later, Hines officially backed out of the stunt."

From that moment on, there was an onslaught of unsuccessful tries at catching a ball dropped from the Washington Monument. Another man, not a ballplayer, attempted to catch a ball and failed, breaking his hand. Others tried, but without success.

Baseball players, especially after a few drinks at their local watering hole, were intrigued by this challenge. A number of visiting teams' players in town to play the Washington Senators also joined in the discussion as to whether a ball dropped from the top of the monument could be caught; many believed it impossible. Cap Anson, the opinionated captain of the Chicago Cubs, took the opposite position. He was so adamant in his belief that a baseball could be caught from such an extreme height that he became involved in a heated debate with a Washington businessman that lasted nine years.

On one road trip, Anson was unable to continue on to Washington and had to return to Chicago to deal with an important matter. That evening, Anson's team dined without him in Washington. After dinner, the topic as to whether a ball dropped from the top of the monument could be caught again surfaced. The Cubs catcher Pop Schriver, took the position that Anson was correct, and volunteered to test his captain's theory. The next morning, a group of Cubs players and other spectators made their way to the Washington Monument. The date was August 25, 1894.

Pop Schriver, Chicago Cubs

According to various reports including *The Washington Post*, the *Sporting News,* and at least one baseball book (*Clark Griffith: The Old Fox of Washington Baseball)*, Pop Schriver arguably accomplished this feat on August 25, 1894, when a ball was dropped from a window at the top of the monument by Cubs pitcher and Schriver teammate, Clark Griffith. The first ball descended with such speed that initially it appeared no larger than an aspirin. As it neared Shriver, it appeared to grow immensely in size. "Pop" stepped aside and watched the ball hit the hard ground and bounce above his head.

Ball number two dropped from the window. "Pop" moved under it ready to make the catch, but the ball crashed into his mitt with such force it bounced out. A major disagreement ensued—the ball was caught...no, it wasn't. As the controversy over whether or not the ball stayed in his mitt long enough to qualify as a good catch was underway, a warning shout interrupted the debate and caused a spontaneous fleeing from the grounds. The monument police were spotted as they approached. Arrests were imminent for those caught. The law prohibited such assemblage without having obtained a permit in advance.

Each of the scattering spectators, no doubt, maintained their personal opinions as to the success of the catch.

Gabby Street, Washington Senators

On August 21, 1908, journalist Preston Gibson stood at the top of the Washington Monument and dropped a baseball. Below, Washington Senators catcher Gabby Street stepped aside, unfazed as he watched the first ball plunge over 500 feet to the ground. The ball hit the ground and bounced high above Street's head. Next came ball number two…three…and four; twelve balls in total. Even though Street was using the same catcher's mitt he used for fellow teammate Walter Johnson's exceedingly hard, fastball pitches, he did not attempt a catch. Those watching began to heckle Street, asking if he was going to just watch or was he there to catch a ball.

Ball number thirteen was the charm; it exploded into Gabby's mitt. The catch was good. Gabby Street confided many years later that he was disappointed he hadn't caught the first one.

"Actually, I should have caught the first ball they threw out…Had my mitt on it and dropped it, when I should have held it. I knew then that it could be done, but the winds bothered me until I finally snagged the thirteenth toss."

"I could not see the ball until it had come down some distance," Street told *The Washington Post*. He had less than seven seconds to track and catch it after the ball had been dropped. "I was given a signal when it was thrown, but I would not see it until it was almost halfway down. Then it seemed to me the ball was waving…either hitting the monument or falling so close to it that it was

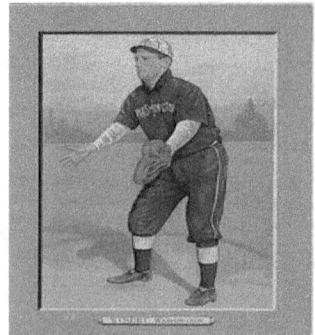

impossible for me to get near it. The ball I caught hit my mitt with terrific force, much greater than any pitched ball I have ever caught, and I have caught some pitchers who are given credit for having wonderful speed. Though my mitt is three or four inches thick, the force of the ball benumbed my hand. I made the catch just as if it were an easy fly ball in a ballgame, only that I held my arms more rigid so as not to have them knocked apart by the force of the ball."

Gabby Street's fame revolved around two events. He managed the Cardinals to the World Series championship in 1931 and, in 1908 became the first person to catch a ball dropped from the top of the Washington Monument. Street's spectacular off-the-diamond catch, like so many baseball legends is debatable. Legend has it that Street missed the first 12 balls, but in 1937 he told *The Washington Post's* sports columnist Shirley Povich, he caught numbers four and thirteen.

Gabby Street finished 1908 as the Senators' catcher and played three more seasons in Washington before Clark Griffith sold him to New York prior to the 1912 season.

World-Record Catch

Today, the accepted *Guinness World Records'* height for a catch is 800 feet. This spectacular catch was made by Chicago Cubs catcher and future Hall of Famer Gabby Hartnett. Hartnett caught a baseball dropped from a blimp on April Fool's Day, April 1, 1930. Reportedly, Hartnett was not wearing any type of protective or catcher's gear when he accomplished the feat; he was wearing a coat and tie.

Over the decades, since Hartnett's record-setting catch, a variety of stories have surfaced. *The New York Times* ran an article and photograph on July 22, 1926, telling the story of how Babe Ruth, running in a vacant field, caught a baseball that was dropped from a plane flying 100 mph at an altitude of 250 feet. The article said the

ball-catching stunt was promoted by the army to advertise a civilian summer camp at Mitchell Field, Garden City, Long Island, NY.

On August 20, 1938, two Cleveland Indians catchers, Frank Pytlak and Hank Helf, caught balls dropped from the 708-foot Terminal Tower in Cleveland. A year later, Joe Sprinz, a former major-league catcher, who was at that time playing for the minor-league Seals, attempted to duplicate Hartnett's feat by catching a ball dropped from a blimp 800 feet above Terminal Island in San Francisco. The ball landed in Sprinz's mitt, but the force of the ball knocked the glove into his unprotected face, breaking his jaw in twelve places, knocking out five of his teeth, and lacerating both lips...and he dropped the ball.

How'd This Guy Get in the Act?

Not to be outdone by the above players, Zack Hample, a professional baseball collector, took the challenge. Hample laid claim to setting a new world's record on Saturday, July 13, 2013, by catching a baseball dropped from a helicopter hovering at 1,050 feet above the ground at LeLacheur Park in Lowell, Massachusetts. Unfortunately, Hample's alleged record-breaking catch did not make the official record books. The folks from *Guinness World Records* declined the invitation to attend and officially witness the event.

For those unfamiliar with Hample, he is the well-known baseball fan who claims to have *caught over 6,000 baseballs* at fifty different major league stadiums over the past twenty-three years. Hample is generally the first person through the gates at every game he attends, wearing the gear of whichever team he plans on soliciting baseballs from. He is also known to switch his allegiance during the course of a game—it's all about collecting balls.

On-the-Mound Wacky & Weird Pitches

With hundreds of thousands of Major League Baseball games played over the decades, a huge number of strange things have taken place. While much of the focus on weird happenings revolve around events that occurred in the field or at home plate, the pitcher's mound has produced its share of the game's daffiest and most unforgettable memories.

Great pitchers use a variety of different baseball pitches, pitch speeds, and movements to gain competitive advantage against the batter. Pitching is an art form, a complicated combination of specific timed movements. Multiple body parts must work in unison to create enough energy to hurl a projectile sixty feet, six inches toward home plate at a high speed.

Every pitcher has a different way of reaching the same end result—some more bizarre and entertaining than others.

Mark "The Bird" Fidrych

As for the pitcher with the most unforgettable and entertaining antics before and after the actual throwing of a pitch, I cast my vote for Mark "The Bird" Fidrych. Fidrych is absolutely one of the quirkiest pitchers to make it to the big leagues, but his behavior had little to do with his pitches. "The Bird's" attraction was what he did between pitches. He was weird...really weird! Just imagine being in the stands and seeing a big league pitcher talking to himself and to the ball. Other odd mannerisms Fidrych displayed included: With the ball in hand, pretending that he was going to throw a dart at a dartboard; getting down on his knees to scratch at the dirt; bending down and smoothing out any cleat marks left by another player; swaggering around the mound after each out; and if an opposing player got a hit, or if he declared that a new baseball had a dent, he'd refuse to throw another pitch until the umpire took that ball out of the game.

Fidrych always drew near-capacity crowds when he was scheduled to pitch. He performed and kept winning ballgames...yes that was "The Bird."

Unfortunately, his career came to an abrupt end after only five seasons in the majors as the result of a rotator cuff injury. At age 54, Mark Fidrych was killed in an accident on his farm in Massachusetts.

Satchel Paige

When speaking of weird things on the mound, "The Bird" Fidrych was certainly entertaining between pitches. But no one could top the "on mound" showmanship of the great Hall of Famer Satchel Paige.

I first met "Satch" in 1953, and he was the funniest and most entertaining ballplayer I ever encountered. "Satch" gave nicknames to all of his pitches. They included his long tom, hurry-up pitch, jump ball, barber, two-hump blooper, and others. Actually, I couldn't tell the difference between his favored "long tom" fastball and his "two-hump blooper."

But what I remember most when Satchel was on the mound was that he had the weirdest windup and delivery that I had ever seen. Satch's most unusual throw was what he called his "hesitation pitch." In this one, he appeared to stop his arm for just a split-second before releasing the ball. He said this motion baffled the batter and threw his timing off.

Satchel Paige was fun to watch. He not only packed ballparks with thousands of fans, he left behind a baseball legacy that will withstand time. Satchel Paige, selected to appear in two All-Star Games, compiled a career record of 28–31 and an ERA of 3.29 in the majors. Inducted into the National Baseball Hall of Fame in 1971, Paige was the first player elected from the Negro Leagues.

Satchel Paige died of an apparent heart attack at his home in Kansas City, Missouri, on June 8, 1982, a month before his seventy-sixth birthday. He is buried in Forest Hill Memorial Park Cemetery in Kansas City.

Eephus pitch

One of the top honors in the weird and wacky "on the mound" category has to be bestowed upon the *Eephus pitch*. The Eephus (blooper) pitch's creator was Rip Sewell of the Pittsburgh Pirates. Sewell would deliver his junk or blooper pitch at a very low speed compared to normal hardball pitches traveling at speeds from 70 to 100 miles per hour. The Eephus only reached speeds of 55 miles per hour or less, and was characterized by an unusually high arcing trajectory of 20-25 feet. The pitch was allegedly given its name by Pittsburgh outfielder, Maurice Van Robays. When Robays was asked what Eephus meant, he responded, *"Eephus ain't nothin' and that's what that ball is."* (It appears that every pitcher throwing this type of pitch has created his own name for it.) Following are two of the Eephus pitch's best known stories:

1946 All-Star Game

In 1946, Pittsburgh Pirates pitcher Rip Sewell successfully pitched his way through the National League, racking up a 3.36 ERA and won a slot on the National League's All-Star team. Sewell, primarily relying on his unique Eephus pitch for the past four years, had mowed down the majority of batters he faced. Despite starting over 100 games with the Eephus in his arsenal, Sewell had not allowed a single home run.

Meanwhile in the American League, Ted Williams had returned from serving in World War II and rejoined the Boston Red Sox. Williams had gone on a spectacular hitting spree in the first half of the season, earning him his fourth All-Star selection.

In the eighth inning of the All-Star Game, with the American League in front by a score of 8-0, Ted Williams stepped into the batter's box for his final time at-bat, with Sewell on the mound. Williams had been forewarned by Sewell that he was going to throw the Eephus, and when Sewell delivered the first one, Williams fouled it off. Sewell threw two more pitches. Then came the fourth pitch—an Eephus. Ready this time, Williams took a running start, stepped well in front of the batter's box, and unleashed his mighty swing. He made perfect contact and hit the ball solidly for a Ted Williams home run.

This hit by Williams was the only home run ever hit off of Sewell's infamous Eephus blooper. As Williams rounded the bases, Sewell let him know the only reason Ted managed to hit his homer was because he had told him it was coming.

Funky Pitch—Funky Name

As the Eephus pitch increased in popularity, more and more pitchers commenced to throw this difficult to hit blooper. Along the way, those pitchers changed the name of the pitch and gave it a name of their own. For example, Dave Steib named it his "Dead Fish"; Bill Lee called it his "Spaceball" or "Leephus" and Dave LaRoche settled on the name, "LaLob." And, who could forget the "Folly Floater"?

Folly Floater

In 1969, Steve Hamilton of the New York Yankees, refined the delivery of his "Folly Floater." Hamilton perfected the effectiveness of his pitch by stepping toward the plate, making his body hesitate, and then as he released the ball, it moved towards the plate in a slow high arc. The pitch delighted spectators and infuriated batters.

On June 24, 1970, pitching for the Yankees, Hamilton threw his "Folly Floater" to Tony Horton of the Cleveland Indians. Horton swung and missed the first ball, then fouled out to the catcher on the second pitch. Returning to the dugout, Horton threw his cap and bat into the air, and crawled the last few steps to the dugout. The crowd roared, and everyone assumed it was a joke. Later, people wondered if it was really a joke.

In 1971, when Hamilton threw the pitch for the first time in the National League, the umpire ruled it illegal, saying, *"This is no halfway league."*

Author's Note

Even after eleven chapters of amazing and zany baseball stories, there is still so much about Major League Baseball and its cast of characters that needs to be told. I feel compelled to continue sharing with you more of the spectacular happenings I witnessed on the field at Griffith Stadium, and to make you privy to a few of the stories that held me spellbound during those special times I spent listening to a variety of team managers, coaches, and players giving their insights on America's greatest game.

In *Baseball's Greatest Hits & Misses, Volume II,* I dip into a few matters that did not directly involve me, but that I consider essential to keeping the spirit of Major League Baseball alive today.

I have compiled a number of amazing and true stories like the scandal that almost destroyed baseball, the pitcher who won a game without throwing a single pitch, MLB's worst trades in history, inspirational stories of a one-legged pitcher and one-arm outfielder, two of the most solemn moments in MLB history, and more.

I doubt if any home run ever has generated more interest or controversy than the "called shot" home run that Babe Ruth hit in Wrigley Field in Chicago during the 1932 World Series. Even today, baseball fans everywhere love to talk, argue and search for the correct answer:

"Did Babe Ruth really call the home run shot he hit in the 1932 World Series?"

During my time at Griffith Stadium in the early 1950s, and when the Yankees were in town, I frequently would ask Bill Dickey, the Yankees' great Hall of Fame catcher—who played seven seasons with Babe Ruth—to tell me about "The Babe." When I asked Bill about the "called shot," he looked at me, smiled, and replied...

The rest of this story and more in *Baseball's Greatest Hits & Misses, Volume II.*

Enjoy!

Jack L. Hayes

About the Author

JACK L. HAYES possesses a highly diversified and rather unique background; as a teenager, he served as a professional batboy for seven Major League Baseball teams, and rubbed elbows with some of the greatest players of all time, including Mickey Mantle, Satchel Paige, Ted Williams, and dozens of other immortal stars.

As an adult, Jack served as CEO of his management consulting firm, Jack L. Hayes International, Inc. for thirty years, and his company has been retained by some of the finest corporations in the United States, Canada, Europe, New Zealand, and South America. Jack, as an internationally recognized authority on business crime and loss prevention, has also consulted with the New York Stock Exchange, United States Marine Corps, and U.S. Navy. He has testified in Federal and State Criminal and Civil Courts as an expert witness on internal and external theft and dishonesty.

Jack is an award-winning published author of four non-fiction books (two on Major League Baseball and two business-related). He has produced 180 minutes of award-winning training videos, served as a regular columnist for two trade magazines, published a subscription newsletter for 22 years; been quoted in numerous newspapers and participated in radio and TV shows. Jack has self-published a variety of educational workbooks and motivational materials. He has lectured on numerous occasions before national and international business audiences, and given presentations on baseball on cruise ships and before various baseball clubs.

Jack and his wife Darlene, live in Central Florida.

PHOTO CREDITS

Page #	PHOTO	CREDIT/REFERENCE
10	Griffith Stadium	historypressblog
16	Bobby Thomson's home run	slicethelife.com
17	Mickey Mantle's Titanic 565 Foot Home Run	Associated Press
20	Bill Mazeroski homer	Getty Images
22	Kirk Gibson's homer	Associated Press
24	Joe Carter's homer	coololdphotos.com
37	Jimmy St. Vrain	baseballhistorydaily.com
41	Germany Schaefer	Library of Congress
47	Neal Ball, Unassisted triple play	National Baseball Hall of Fame
50	Walter Carlisle	Wikipedia
53	Vassar College's "The Resolutes"	Vassar College Library
54	Bloomer girl	printerest.com
56	Lizzie Arlington	Gilbert & Bacon
59	Lizzie Murphy	newenglandhistoricalsociety
61	Marcenia "Toni" Stone	Wikipedia
65 & 67	Jackie Mitchell (2 photos)	todayifoundout.com

74	MLB team mascots	Bleachereport.com
76	Jackie Price	didthetribewinlastnight.com
77	Nick Altrock	pinterest.com
80	Eddie Gaedel	birthmoviesdeath.com
84	Jim Piersall's 100th homer	Associated Press
89	Smead Jolley	bigbadbaseball.blogspot.com
91	Bill Buckner	Associated Press
92	Fred Snodgrass	pinterest.com
94	Mickey Owen's Muff	unclemikesmusings.blogspot.com
96	Babe Ruth's failed steal	Wikipedia
100	Fred Merkle	nytimes.com
105	Fred Merkle Memorial	watertownhistory.org
108	Willie Mays "The Catch"	pinterest.com
110	Ron Swoboda's catch	nola.com
111	Ken Griffey Jr's catch that robbed Barfield	bleacherreport.com
112	Gary Matthews' tremendous vertical leaping catch	plus.google.com
112	Reed Johnson's catch	Mlb.com
116	Gabby Street, Washington Senators	pinterest.com
116	Baseball with date Aug. 21, 1908	whaleswoldwideblakrak.blogspot.com
117	Babe Ruth and airplane	stuffnobodycaresabout.com
119	Mark Fidrych	Wikipedia
120	Satchel Paige	Time.com

END NOTES

1 Stengel would later be criticized for his failing to place Ford in the pitcher's rotation so that he would be available to start three times. This misjudgment would later play an instrumental role in the firing of Casey Stengel as the Yankees' manager, after twelve seasons consisting of ten pennant wins.

2 This story was first reported in The Detroit Free Press (1906). It also appeared to take life later by being quoted in at least two baseball books and on the Internet. Various reports cite that Davy Jones of the 1902 Chicago Cubs, told the late baseball historian Larry Ritter, the following story that was quoted in Ritter's book, The Glory of Their Times, thus adding creditability to the possibility that this really weird event may have actually happened.

3 Rule 7.08(i): "Any runner is out when — after he has acquired legal possession of a base; he runs the bases in reverse order for the purpose of confusing the defense or making a travesty of the game. The umpire shall immediately call "Time" and declare the runner out." The ruling was that Segura never intended to confuse the Cubs or make a travesty of the game. He just made a mistake, so on that individual play Segura was ruled safe.

4 There is at least one other report that Germany Schaefer, while playing with the Detroit Tigers, also stole first base against Cleveland in 1908. However, this incident could not be substantiated.

5 Professional baseball leagues use an official "score keeping method" to officially make a record of each game. Scorekeeping is generally done on a printed scorecard and, while official scorers must adhere precisely to one of the few different scorekeeping notations, so that a complete and accurate accounting of the game is recorded. For scoring purposes each defensive position is referred to by number.

Pitcher = 1 Catcher = 2 1st base = 3 2nd base = 4 3rd base = 5 shortstop = 6 left field = 7 center field = 8 right field = 9

Therefore, a 4-5-4 triple play means the ball was initially hit to the second baseman (4), who then threw the ball to the third baseman (5), who then threw the ball back to the second baseman (4).

6 Story told by Schaefer's teammate, Davy Jones, in the book, The Glory of Their Times.

7 Check out this amazing video of Jackie Price performing a few of his unbelievable feats: http://www.baseball-almanac.com/players/videos.php?p=priceja01

8 Balk: The briefest definition of a balk is anytime there is a runner, or runners on base, and the pitcher, while touching the mound's rubber/plate, makes any motion naturally associated with his/her pitch and fails to make such delivery. There are many actions that can result in a balk. When runners are on base and a balk is called, all runners advance one base. (MLB Official Rule, 8.05)

9 Retrosheet is a non-profit organization whose website features major league baseball box scores and play-by-play narratives for almost every contest from 1871–1872, 1874, 1911 National League, and since 1918. It also includes scores from every Major League Baseball game played since the 1871 season, as well as all All-Star,

League Championship Series and World Series games. Retrosheet was founded in 1989 by Dr. David Smith, a biology professor at the University of Delaware.

10 *Check it out: BB Moments: Willie Mays' Catch | MLB.com*

11 *Videos available on the Internet.*

12 *Check out Kevin Mitchell's amazing catch on: www.mlb.com/Kevin Mitchell makes unbelievable catch*

13 *Click on link, Swoboda makes the catch\MLB.com*

14 *Check it out, click on link: http://m.mlb.com/griffey-reaches-over-the-fence-to-rob-barfield*

15 *Check it out: http://m.mlb.com/matthews-defies-gravity-to-make-the-catch*

16 *Check it out: http://m.mlb.com/johnson-robs-fielder-of-a-grand-slam*

www.ingramcontent.com/pod-product-compliance
Lightning Source LLC
LaVergne TN
LVHW021514080426
835509LV00018B/2513